SOUL TRAVELER

SOUL TRAVELER

A GUIDE TO OUT-OF-BODY EXPERIENCES AND THE WONDERS BEYOND

ALBERT TAYLOR

A DUTTON BOOK

DUTTON
Published by the Penguin Group
Penguin Putnam Inc., 375 Hudson Street, New York, New York 10014, U.S.A.
Penguin Books Ltd, 27 Wrights Lane, London W8 5TZ, England
Penguin Books Australia Ltd, Ringwood, Victoria, Australia
Penguin Books Canada Ltd, 10 Alcorn Avenue, Toronto, Ontario, Canada M4V 3B2
Penguin Books (N.Z.) Ltd, 182–190 Wairau Road, Auckland 10, New Zealand

Penguin Books Ltd, Registered Offices: Harmondsworth, Middlesex, England

Published by Dutton, an imprint of Dutton NAL, a member of Penguin Putnam Inc.
Originally published in a different version by Verity Press.

First Dutton Printing, September, 1998
10 9 8 7 6 5 4 3 2 1

LIBRARY OF CONGRESS CATALOGING-IN-PUBLICATION DATA:

Taylor, Albert.
Soul traveler : a guide to out-of-body experiences and the wonders beyond / Albert Taylor.
p. cm.
Originally published: Covina, CA : Verity Press, 1996.
Includes bibliographical references.
ISBN 0-525-94447-8
1. Astral projection. I. Title.
[BF1389.A7T39 1998]
133.9'5—dc21 98-21613
CIP

Printed in the United States of America
Designed by Leonard Telesca
Set in Sabon

This book is printed on acid-free paper. 

To my son

DEVON

Without your love I would not have had the courage to venture as far as I did.
You are my dream child, and my shining star.
All my love forever, Dad.

MY SPECIAL THANKS TO:

Shirley MacLaine
Beatrice Scott
Jack Houck
Pat Lewis
Kim Craven
Dr. Carole Carbone
Susan Walker
IANDS
Luz Virgen
Daryll Ford
Constance Ray
Nancy Henderson
The Learning Light Foundation
Catherine Coleman
and Otto-Matic

CONTENTS

FOREWORD

Albert Taylor believes that he is a normal person, but he is *not*. Oh, sure, he is emotionally and mentally healthy, pays his taxes and knows his zip code. He's friendly to people and pets, tells a good joke and maintains a straight-arrow list of personal habits. But no, Albert Taylor is not normal.

It is not normal to be a good Catholic altar boy and have your grandmother describe your nightly flying dreams as witches' rides. It is not normal to single-handedly raise kids from diapers through diplomas and, without maternal influence, have them turn out terrific. It is not normal to be an African-American NASA space engineer. And for that matter, it is not normal to be an African-American on the metaphysics lecture circuit. No, Albert Taylor is not normal. Albert Taylor is *extraordinary*.

Friendship notwithstanding, none of this would matter to me if Albert wasn't on to something that has the glorious potential to enhance the human condition: the out-of-body experience. Albert has not written *Soul Traveler* out of some self-serving agenda. He wrote this book to teach others how to stretch the limits of their awareness beyond the laws of gravity and motion, to experience unencumbered flight. It was his desire to help others, not his engineering expertise, which drew me to Albert Taylor's work. But who better to validate the existence of these capacities than an aeronautical engineer?

I am very familiar with what it feels like to be out of my body, both within the context of the near-death experience that I had in 1970 and within the context of numerous out-of-body experiences I've had in the past thirty years. As a social worker immersed in the medical world, I know how important it is to have solid validation on both counts. It means that maybe one is *not* crazy, hallucinating, fibbing, imagining, dreaming, or any of the other dismissive rationales posed by skeptics. As I wrote in my book *After the Light: The Spiritual Path to Purpose*, the validation I needed for my own near-death experience came from a flat-lining patient of mine, who during her own near-death experience observed a tennis shoe in a remote spot on a hospital window ledge.

In the more than twenty years since this incident, more validation has come to me in the form of countless out-of-body experiences reported to me by trauma patients, burn victims, women in labor and delivery, mountain climbers who have fallen from great heights, marathon runners who found themselves at treetop level looking down on their still running physical selves, people in prayer or meditation, the bereaved, or people like Albert, who have an innate ability to leave their bodies almost at will.

Albert's ability to guide you toward an out-of-body experience will not only free you from earthly limitations, it will also demonstrate that we as human beings are as much spirit as flesh. To *hope* that this aspect of ourselves exists is a common emotional reaction to life's challenges. To have *faith* that this aspect of ourselves exists is what drives people to join churches and temples. To *know* that this aspect of ourselves exists is to have practiced the simple lessons described in *Soul Traveler*. And when you've done so, when you have experienced firsthand the mysterious, enlightening, and awesome freedom of journeying out of your body, consider looking up at the night sky and thanking God for Albert Taylor, space engineer, for teaching us how to touch the stars.

—Kimberly Clark Sharp, author of *After the Light*

INTRODUCTION

Some men see things that are, and ask why. I dream of things that never were, and ask why not.

—John F. Kennedy

Is there life beyond death? Does the soul really exist? Are angels and ghosts real? Are these spiritual beings helping to shape mankind's destiny?

Within these pages I describe my soul travels, also known as out-of-body experiences, and because of them I believe I have found some answers to these questions.

First, I must say that I am not what you would call a religious person. Although I was baptized Catholic and served as an altar boy, I have not attended church regularly in years. Also, my life has not been filled with psychic occurrences. However, I have experienced, since the age of four, a type of "paralysis" during the night and early morning. "The witches are riding you!" is what my grandmother would always say. This state of feeling paralyzed, I have found out, was my personal doorway to what may be the "ultimate truth."

What is this strange feeling? All my life, as far back as I can remember, I have had a peculiar sensation that I once dreaded. Often I would wake up fully aware of my surroundings; I could hear and see, but I was incapable of moving. I felt paralyzed! I call this the "paralysis state." This same phenomenon happened to my mother and my cousin Robert, and we *all* hated it!

For years I "suffered" with this "affliction." I found out early on that during the paralysis I was capable only of moaning aloud, nothing more. I call this the "abort sequence." After I was married, my wife became so accustomed to this that she would nudge me with her elbow to wake me. I would then be capable of moving my body again.

I didn't have a clue as to how close I was to achieving an "out-of-body experience." This is one term that is currently used—"astral projection" and "going exterior" are others—but I prefer to call it "soul travel." I use this term for a variety of reasons, one being because it is used by a group known as the Eckankar Society, but more on that later.

Another peculiar thing that happened during sleep is what I used to call "waking up in my dreams." Although sound asleep, I became cognizant that I was dreaming, or at least aware of what I thought was a dream. Scientific and metaphysical circles refer to this as "lucid dreaming." After waking up in my dream, I had the ability to change the dream! Sometimes I would fly. Other times I explored my surroundings. Keeping my thoughts focused wasn't always easy, but when I did, it was always exciting.

These two common occurrences, the paralysis state and waking up in my dreams, remained unconnected for most of my childhood and adult life.

One evening I rented the movie *Out on a Limb*, starring Shirley MacLaine. The film had a profound impact on me, one that I did not fully understand at that time. At the end of the film Shirley MacLaine has an out-of-body experience resulting from a series of spiritual events. I was so affected by this movie that I wrote her a letter (which I never mailed). It read:

> *Dear Shirley MacLaine,*
>
> *I am not in the habit of writing or contacting celebrities as a fan or otherwise. But writing to you is something I feel compelled to do.*
>
> *Recently my wife and I viewed your film* Out on a Limb *on video, after which we both were deeply affected. It has been two weeks since then, and I still feel undeniably affected by this film.*
>
> *Presently, I am an engineer on NASA's Space Station Freedom program, and have worked in aerospace for the last two decades on various government classified and nonclassified programs. I consider myself lucky to have been exposed to projects that most Americans won't hear about for years to come, if ever.*
>
> *All my life I have been and continue to be inter-*

ested in astronomy, space travel, UFOs, and psychic phenomena. I don't want you to get the impression that my only interest is in space-related areas. I just wanted to give you an idea of my background, in hopes of adding some credibility to this letter.

Well, to make a long story short, I am seeking knowledge about life—past, present, and future. I'd like to know more about astral projection. I'd like to know more about the Force that is in and around us. I would like to discover the connection between out-of-body experiences and this Force.

In conclusion, I wanted to tell you that I applaud your courage in coming forth with your discoveries. In doing so, you have subjected yourself to ridicule among your peers and the media. It seems to me that you have put everything on the line for what may be the ultimate truth. So if you can find time in your busy schedule, I would appreciate suggestions from you on a direction or path to follow.

Sincerely,
Albert Taylor Jr.

I became intrigued with the thought of having my own out-of-body experience. I shared my interest with my close friend, Kim, who suggested I take a metaphysics course taught by Dr. H. at the local college. Having had a near-death experience and having witnessed a host of psychic occurrences, Dr. H. was driven to teach classes that focused on spiritual awareness and enlightenment.

My wife and I signed up for the first part of a series of lecture/workshops that Dr. H. had developed and taught.

During one of the classes Dr. H. asked a question that would change my life. She asked if anyone ever felt *paralyzed* at night after lying down to sleep. I had thought the paralysis was mine alone (well, along with my mother and cousin Robert)! Dr. H. began to describe how this paralysis was related to out-of-body experiences. At first I doubted her because I *knew* that I had not had an out-of-body experience.

Dr. H. then said that dreams of flying may very well be out-of-body experiences. I thought, "No way! I fly all the time!" I left the class both puzzled and excited. Could this be true? Were my dreams of flying out-of-body experiences?

I went out and bought every book I could find on out-of-body experiences and astral projection. Robert Monroe's *Journeys Out of the Body* and Dr. Keith Harary and Pamela Weintraub's *Out of Body Experiences,* were two out of the many I read.

Monroe's book in particular fascinated and scared me. He kept telling of disembodied entities in his book. That struck a deep chord of fear within me. I was afraid of ghosts, even though I had no justifiable reason.

Yet his book also triggered memories. I recalled one time, when I was about four years old, that while feeling paralyzed, a figure sat at the end of my bed and whispered my name.

"Alllberrrt!"

Another time, around the age of seven, I remember

lying at the foot of my parents' bed, watching the *Louis Lomax Show*. Lomax was interviewing a man who claimed to have captured the ghostly images of monks praying in a medieval English cathedral. The image of blurry, soft white figures kneeling among the cathedral pews scared me so much I refused to go to bed. Finally my mother sent me to bed clutching a set of Catholic rosary beads close to my chest, and reciting the "Hail Mary" prayer over and over again. I had no idea why I had such a strong fear of ghosts, entities, or spirits. After all, it's not as if such things exist, right?

I soon learned that fear would be the bars in a prison of my own creation. If I wanted to soul travel, I would have to break free of that prison. Only then could I explore the limitless world beyond the constraints of everyday life.

SOUL TRAVELER

1
AIRBORNE

I want to fly more than anything else in the world!

—Richard Bach, *Jonathan Livingston Seagull*

In February 1993, I visited my regular physician in hopes of finding possible physical reasons for the paralysis I felt so often. As I sat there in the examination room, I rehearsed how I was going to phrase my questions.

"Doctor, have you ever had a patient who couldn't get up while sleeping?" (The answer to this would likely be: "Yes, all of them.")

"Doctor, I lose control of my body at night." (Sounds like demonic possession.)

"Hey Doc, I have concerns about being paralyzed." (This sounds like paranoia.)

"Good afternoon, Doctor! I've been meaning to tell you about my paralysis." (A bit too casual.)

Just then the doctor walked into the room. "Hello, Mr. Taylor," she said. "How are you?"

She proceeded to check me over. During the exam she asked so many questions, I hardly got a word in edgewise. Finally my chance came.

"Doctor," I said. "Have you ever awakened in the middle of the night feeling paralyzed?"

She looked at me and smiled. "Don't worry about it, that happens to me sometimes. You'll be all right."

"But I'm not—"

"You're in good health, Mr. Taylor. See you in three months." She turned and walked out. So much for the wisdom of the medical world.

Soon afterward I would have another of these bouts of paralysis. The difference this time, though, was that I was curious about experiencing an out-of-body experience. If I tried—in whatever way I was supposed to try—would feeling paralyzed lead to astral projection? In a diary that I started keeping, I recorded for the first time what actually happened.

March 14, 1993

At ten o'clock, I went to bed a little afraid. I drifted off to sleep, not really knowing what I should do to achieve an out-of-body experience. I really wasn't sure what if anything to do except sleep.

I must have drifted off, because the next thing I knew, I was lying on the bed in that odd state of paralysis.

Then, without warning, something grabbed my arm. Startled, I fought my way out of the paralysis, partially sat up on the bed, and looked at the clock. It was three A.M.

That certainly didn't accomplish anything. Except for the strange sensation of feeling my arm grabbed, the session might have been any one of hundreds over the years. All during the next day I thought the matter over, determined that on my next try I was going to get somewhere. I'd just have to push through the paralysis and whatever grabbed me.

March 15, 1993

I settled into bed at nine-thirty, moderately tired. I relaxed my body and surrounded myself with white light as suggested in some of the astral projection books I'd read. I now refer to fearful preparation as training wheels, since a number of the tools and techniques I used in the beginning were meant to assist me like the extra wheels on a child's bike. After a certain amount of practice I no longer needed them.

I soon drifted off into a light sleep, and the next thing I knew I was flying. The sensation was like past ones I'd had, but I was flying better and faster than I'd ever flown. I thought to myself, "Wow, I did it!"

Dr. H. had suggested I visit her if I ever left my body, and I made up my mind to do so. I changed directions and zipped off. On the way there, I experimented with speed and altitude. I thought, "Speed up," and I did. I thought, "Fly higher," and I did. Down below I saw houses, trees, and neighborhood streets, only they melted together into one continuous blur. Never had I traveled so fast. No car, train, or plane could match this speed. I slowed my velocity—and became aware that I was being drawn down toward the roof of a house that was rapidly looming larger.

Into the house I went. I entered a room through a wall and floated up to the foot of a bed. I thought that I was in a hospital room because a bright white figure, whom I thought to be a nurse, was standing next to the person in the bed. As I approached the foot of the bed, the white figure backed away. Dr. H. was lying on the bed; she did not appear to be awake. Suddenly, without moving, I mentally heard her say, "Congratulations, Al, you did it."

"I know," I replied.

We were communicating with more than just words. Not only could I hear her voice, but I felt the mood in which she said it. I also noticed that she and her husband did not sleep in the same bed. I thought this would be something worth verifying when I saw her physically, because I still wasn't convinced that I was really there. I could be dreaming. I experienced a quick visual shift, some rapid movement, and found myself back in bed. I sat up leaning on my elbows and thought, "That was great!" I turned over on my side and fell asleep.

When I awoke the next morning, I thought over what had happened. Was I dreaming? How could Dr. H. see and hear me? I would later learn that we are mind, body, and soul and the soul can communicate with other souls without the mind being aware of the exchange. The mind is the conscious part of us that interacts with the everyday material world.

For some reason, when the body falls asleep, the soul comes to the forefront of consciousness. But in the waking world the mind or personality self is the dominant state. Later I would find out that we are conscious and aware on many other nonphysical levels as well. And, it is possible for each of us to functionally connect these states of awareness. Some people are born with this type of ability and we generally refer to them as psychic or insightful. Others are capable of doing this through meditation. And still others connect after the body falls asleep, like me. If a person were capable of being in constant connection with the soul at all levels, I believe the majority of our fears would have very little meaning.

Later that week my wife and I attended another metaphysics class. I could hardly wait to talk to Dr. H., but I held back until the break. Greeting her, I asked, "So Dr. H., did anything happen over the weekend?"

She said she remembered seeing me in a dream but could not recall the details. Plus, she remembered my turning away from her as if I was leaving. I then began to describe her bedroom, asking if she and her husband slept in separate beds. Dr. H. looked at me and smiled. "Yes, that is correct."

I wondered if the entire episode was just a weird coincidence. Dr. H. remembered me only in a dream, and I didn't want to read more into it than that. I'd been hoping that she would have remembered a little more.

March 20, 1993

That night I decided not to attempt an out-of-body experience. I attempted to surround myself with white light, because I was too fearful. Nothing happened before I fell asleep, but later I woke up in the middle of the night vibrating. I crossed my arms, turned over on my left side, and fell asleep.

The vibrations, or "vibes," I had felt numerous times, but I'd always thought they were earth tremors. Living in California, I didn't pay much attention to the experiences at first, but in time I realized that the vibrations were another part of the astral experience. I would later discover that the vibrations are a signal that my consciousness is transitioning to a higher level of reality. The astral plane, as metaphysicians refer to it, is the next level above the physical. When I finally learned to control the vibrations, I was able to access planes of consciousness beyond the astral. It appears that my soul body vibrates or oscillates at a particular rate. The nonphysical beings that inhabit these realms also appear to be at various vibrational states. I wonder if the more an individual spirit evolves, the higher the soul consciousness vibrates. And are angels and other saintly beings at extreme levels of vibrational consciousness?

Two days later, I experienced the same vibrations. This happened during a nap around four o'clock. I relaxed until I finally dropped off, then woke a short while later with my body vibrating. I looked for signs of an earthquake, but there were none. The sensation of vibrating was happening on a level beyond the physical.

March 28, 1993

I began to suspect that relaxation may be an important key to experiencing the vibrations. So I bought a tape to aid me in my experiments. The tape instructed me to visualize relaxing every muscle in my body, one at a time. I performed the exercises and drifted off into a light sleep. Shortly thereafter I woke and noticed the tape was half over (about twenty minutes had passed). I took off the headphones and fell asleep.

I awoke in what I'd always considered a lucid dream. I was walking on a sidewalk. I stopped suddenly because I was puzzled as to how I got there. I then thought, "Is this a dream?"

In the past, when I became lucid in my dreams, I would perform a simple test. I would attempt to fly low over the ground. Now I focused my thoughts, leaned forward, and I began flying slowly over the sidewalk.

I stood up, looked around, and thought, "I did it again." I continued to check out my surroundings, which were illuminated by a strange glow. It was neither dark nor daylight, more like an eerie dusk. In addition, the lighting did not appear to have a single source. I took off flying over the city—or *a* city, I had no idea where I was.

Soon I was flying over a neighborhood. Below me was what looked like a swimming pool. Suddenly an idea came to me. I decided to experiment. I flew right into the water. At first I held my breath—because I didn't want to be the first to drown astrally. At last I decided to take in a breath. I could feel cool water all around me, and the coolness came into me as I inhaled. I thought, "This is incredible."

I became aware that two or three figures were standing just beyond the edge of the pool, slightly beyond my vision. I felt as if the figures were observing me, like teachers monitoring a playground. Fearful of a possible encounter, I flew out of the water and into the sky. Wherever I was, I could see many rooftops close together.

Suddenly, there was a loud crash. I opened my physical eyes, sat up in bed, and blurted out, "Jesus!"

My wife stood at the end of the bed, smiling sheepishly. "Sorry," she said. "I dropped the flashlight."

March 30, 1993

Not for another week would I attempt another out-of-body experience. I lay flat on my back around midnight, trying to relax and clear my mind. After what felt like an eternity, I began to feel a low-level tingling slowly increase to a full-blown vibration. I was a little surprised because this was the first time I had started the vibrations before falling asleep, so I really didn't know what to expect.

During this shaking I felt several strong, jarring surges, and fear set in. I crossed my arms, turned over on my left side, and fell asleep.

April 11, 1993

Around three-thirty A.M. I woke up and had difficulty going back to sleep, so I decided to attempt to reach the vibration state with the help of a relaxation tape. Halfway through I stopped the tape and turned over. Soon I felt myself begin vibrating. I turned over on my back and tried to increase the trembling. The vibes started to surge from deep within me like the foreshocks of an earthquake—with my head the epicenter.

I thought about floating upward. Just like that, I felt the top of my head rubbing against the headboard of our bed. The headboard had begun to slide downward! I could actually feel the vinyl surface moving past me, or was I moving past it?

Then suddenly I could see, but my physical eyes were not open. I noticed an eerie, nondirectional lighting radiating inside our bedroom. There was also an intermittent, high-volume buzzing sound. I thought to myself, "Is this it?" I decided to get up physically, but I could not move an inch! I was paralyzed! This realization caught me completely off guard. This was the first time that I had experienced the paralysis without sleeping first, then waking up in it.

Without warning, a humanoid shape appeared about eighteen inches away from me. Startled, I mentally told it to move away. It did not respond, though it did become increasingly transparent.

I panicked! I began moaning, hoping that my wife would wake me up, which she did. I noticed that the lighting in the room changed as I reconnected with my body.

After waking, I told my wife about the ghostly apparition. She said I had not moved physically, and when she nudged me awake, my head was approximately nine inches from the headboard. I had been about that far away from the headboard before I fell asleep.

Thinking about it afterward, I decided I hadn't exactly been afraid of the figure near me. I think that the buzzing sound, the lighting, floating into the air, the paralysis, and finally the figure all overwhelmed me. My wife had described my head as being physically nine inches away from the headboard, yet I had felt the uneven button tucking of the vinyl surface. Did I astral project out of the top of my head?

I've read in various books that this is very common, though I'm not sure I would use the word *common.* I have also read in books on Hindu religions, such as the Paramahansa Yogananda's book, *Autobiography of a Yogi,* that something called a "crown chakra" is at the top of the head. I wonder if this may have something to do with my leaving the body that way. Whatever helps to create the exit for my soul appears to happen naturally. After numerous repeats of the leaving through the top of the head, I have substituted the word *natural* for *common.*

April 24, 1993

A week later, another astral sensation occurred, though it was fleeting. I decided to use the relaxation tape again. While I was lying there, feeling very relaxed, a brilliant light flashed across my eyelids. It was blue and was accompanied by a zipping or buzzing sound. I briefly wondered what to make of this, then fell asleep.

My next full-blown experience took place the following week. Again I would not leave the bedroom, but my astral world was expanding all the same.

May 1, 1993

I woke up feeling paralyzed, a little frightened, but talked myself out of it. I tried a different way to leave this time. I remembered reading in Robert Monroe's book *Journeys out of the Body* that an alternate way to leave the body was to "roll out." I thought of rolling over, and I did. Then I realized I was looking down at my wife's face. I was floating about twelve inches or so directly above her. I also sensed a presence in the room, but it seemed content to stay near the television.

I tried to stand up, feeling for the blanket with my *"astral feet."* That's when I noticed the blankets weren't solid; my foot pushed through them with very little effort. Intrigued, I felt the vinyl surface of the waterbed mattress, and with the slightest pressure I was able to push through to the heated water underneath. The plywood support panel underneath the mattress resisted at first, then gave way to my probing foot.

Down through the plywood I pushed to the carpet below. I couldn't believe it. I was standing in the middle of the bed moving my astral feet across the carpet! I was looking around the room when the thought of venturing farther crossed my mind. With that thought, however, I must have drifted into a non-lucid dream state, but all is blank after that.

It was a strange way to end an out-of-body experience. Normally I remembered returning, but not this time. Could it be that my jaunts were being guided by some unseen force, which was allowing me to experience out-of-body experiences in small doses at a time?

I wonder if the majority of people have out-of-body experiences but lose consciousness or drift into the "normal" dream state and forget their experiences, as I must have done. An important key to this question might be to remain consciously aware, lucid and present in the moment in order to retain the memory of the out-of-body experience upon waking, but this appears to be easier said than done. This particular idea is what prompted me to develop the interrupted sleep technique. With this technique my consciousness was capable of staying aware while my physical body drifted off to sleep. One of the strangest things I have experienced while performing the interrupted sleep technique is to hear someone snoring, and find out that it is me.

Some months later I would have another variation on my explorations within the safety of my bedroom. This time, though, would point the way toward further enlightenment: that my astral body could be quite unlike my physical one.

June 7, 1994

I woke up in the paralysis state and, without my prodding, the lower half of my body began to float. Like the hinged lid of a music box, my astral body moved up and my head rotated backward! The soles of my astral feet were pointing straight at the ceiling. I was upside down and facing backward, but my astral head was still connected to my physical head. I hung there upside down staring at the headboard of our bed. I couldn't seem to break free, so I gave up and reconnected.

2

BUZZING BEES

Who maketh the clouds his chariot: who walketh upon the wings of the wind . . .

—Psalms 104:3–4

Dr. H. has been a tremendous resource of information and shared many techniques as well. In this early stage she told me she taught another class that specifically focused on out-of-body experiences and suggested I attend. She also invited me to join her at an International Association of Near Death Studies (IANDS) group meeting held in Santa Fe Springs, California.

The class turned out to be a great help. I not only learned about historically documented cases, but met individuals eager to have experiences similar to mine. After the third and final out-of-body class, I told Dr. H. how much I disliked the feeling of paralysis and asked if she had any pointers on controlling or tolerating it.

Her advice was wonderfully simple. "When you feel paralyzed, just think of moving your little finger; you'll reconnect," she said. With this added bit of information, I would be able to reconnect with my body with very little effort. There'd be no more panic, and no more fighting my way out of it. Because of Dr. H., I stopped dreading the feeling of paralysis and actually looked forward to it.

In July 1993, I attended my first IANDS group meeting. The firsthand accounts of its members' near-death experiences were fascinating. One woman, Rosanna, had three near-death experiences as the result of a liver disease. Another woman had a car accident that forced her and her son (a passenger) to have simultaneous near-death experiences.

I was uneasy about sharing my out-of-body experiences. After all, these people had experienced death, while I was only performing exploratory missions. Yet as a result of the three near-death experiences Rosanna continues to have conscious, controlled out-of-body experiences, far more often than anyone else the members knew. I had to meet her. To make a long story short, Rosanna and I met and I felt very comfortable with her and shared some of my jaunts. We became good friends, exchanging books, relaxation tapes, and conversation.

I no longer considered myself some kind of wide-eyed weirdo. Whatever was happening to me, my life was expanding onto a new, exciting plane of existence. I was now ready to explore the astral plane, and possibly beyond.

September 26, 1993

Yet, oddly enough, nothing happened for the next three months. Then one night I got up at one-thirty because I couldn't sleep. I stayed up until four-thirty. Shortly after going back to bed I started my own "pre-flight routine" that I've developed since my experiences began.

The out-of-body experience began. I felt my legs floating upward. Marveling at this, I proceeded to move my legs downward and right through the mattress. I kept doing this for a minute or so. Up and down, up and down. My astral legs didn't feel like my physical legs; they felt rubbery or elastic. I could extend them or wrap them around each other, almost like a pretzel. I could also change their size and shape at will.

Then something happened that would permanently alter my out-of-body experiences. The softest, kindest female voice that I have ever heard spoke into my ear.

"Al . . . ?"

I panicked! Someone, or something, was gently holding my arms. Though the grip was more protective than restraining, I initiated the abort sequence, moaning to be woken up. My wife was right on time. I reconnected and sat up.

Not only had I seen, felt, and heard an apparition, it decided to communicate. I guess if it hadn't been aware of my fear of spirits before, it was now! How patient my guides were during my earlier explorations. If only I'd known that something wonderful and totally beyond my imagination was trying to open a dialogue. But as I stated before, fear became a prison of my own creation. I believe the majority of my fearful reactions stem from having grown up conditioned by controlling religious beliefs. My Catholic upbringing primarily taught fear rather than love and faith. I always thought that something nonphysical and intelligent had to be evil! Boy, was I wrong!

The next day, I told a friend at work whom I trust about the strange occurrences. She said I should visit the Eckankar Society. I'd never heard of it. Given the fact I am a native of Southern California, I have since wondered why I hadn't. The main office of the Eckankar Society was located right in Anaheim, California.

That very day I drove over there. Walking in the front door, I interrupted a group of people sitting in a circle in the middle of the room. A middle-aged woman smiled at me, motioning for me to take a seat. After I did, they all closed their eyes and began to sing the strangest song. I joined in softly, trying not to stand out.

After they completed what I now know to be the "Hu," they began to discuss dreams and how they were influenced by spiritual masters. After a while I raised my hand.

"Yes?" the woman asked with curiosity.

I answered. "I've never been here before, and I was wondering what this is all about."

"You fit in so well, we all thought you were an Eckist."

"He even Hu'd with us!" another person remarked.

I was then treated as if I were a long-lost relative. I had

never before been greeted by strangers who openly and genuinely expressed such love. I told them about my experiences and that I was searching for some way to understand them. One woman left the room, returning with a chart.

It depicted the various levels of consciousness. She pointed to the etheric level. The sound associated with that level is "buzzing bees." These people had a chart that listed the sound that I had heard. They then began to explain to me the meaning of Eckankar.

The word means "coworker with God." They believe that is the ultimate destiny of the soul and that this purpose can be achieved only through the lessons learned from numerous reincarnations. One of the men directed me to their in-house library, informing me that I was welcome to take home any of their books or cassette tapes as long as I returned them.

Over the next few months, I was to learn that the Eckankar Society practices a number of spiritual exercises to help a person accomplish a variety of things, including "soul travel." Interestingly, they do not consider themselves to have a soul. "We *are* soul," they profess with conviction.

One book I borrowed from their library was about a man who learned to soul travel. After reading this book, I was inspired to develop the technique of going to bed early and setting an alarm to wake up at one-thirty. Then, get out of bed, stay up for a couple of hours, and do not eat or drink anything except water. Then go back to bed. I eventually called this the interrupted sleep technique or IST for short.

In the Eckankar book the author described waking up in the middle of the night to assist in soul travel. This sounded like what I had experienced the night before. Or was it just a coincidence?

The author continued with instructions on chanting the "Hu" (pronounced like the name Hugh). This was described as a love song to God. The Hu is chanted by taking a deep breath and slowly letting it out through parted lips, singing one long continuous "hu" sound.

A second book listed over a hundred different spiritual exercises to aid a person in psychic achievements—clairvoyance, spiritual healing, past-life regression, and, of course, soul travel.

Later that week I attended the Eckankar World Seminar at the Los Angeles Convention Center. I'd never heard of this group, but to my surprise, there were over two thousand people from all over the world, including Spain, England, Africa, and Germany. And all of them believed in the soul leaving the body.

My primary reason for attending was to meet someone experiencing psychic occurrences similar to mine. To my disappointment, most of the people were merely hoping to achieve soul travel or had their focus in other areas, such as healing and predicting the future or exploring past lives.

The interrupted sleep technique, however, would lead to a new blossoming of astral activity. During a ten-day experiment between October 7 and October 17, 1993, I would have eight hits out of ten tries. I had three out-of-body experiences in one night. Two of them began unlike any of the previous ones.

October 15, 1993

I lay quietly until I became aware of a small scene forming between my eyes. As I stared at the image, it grew larger and larger until suddenly I was standing in it. Nearby was what looked like a neighborhood street corner.

I looked around and realized, as before, that I had no idea where I was. Feeling brave, I asked to see my guide as I had read about in various pieces of metaphysical literature, pointing at a spot ten feet in front of me. I figured that was close enough for a first-time meeting.

I repeated my request, but nothing happened. I thought of my body and wondered how easy it would be to return. Before I could even complete the thought, there was a quick visual shift and rapid movement, and I was slammed back into my body.

I wanted to go back, though. I lay still, and soon there was another picture in what I have learned is my "third eye." I experienced the same sequence of events; the picture grew larger and larger until I stood in it.

This time I leaned forward and flew up into the sky. I felt like Jonathan Livingston Seagull as I soared, appreciating an incredible view of green hillsides dotted with an occasional house or apartment building. Strangely, this prompted an urge to return. I thought of my body, experienced a visual blur, entered, and reconnected.

In earlier flights, before I found out that I was really having an out-of-body experience (I didn't know that it was by pure thought alone that I flew), a fearful thought would occur to me that I might lose altitude or fall, and immediately I would plummet from the sky in a panic. Most of the time I would pull back up just in the nick of time to skip across the ground, like a flat rock on a pond. I would then use my hands to push off the ground and climb skyward again. Other times I would fly at an extremely slow rate a few feet above the ground, unable to speed up or climb. All the while unbeknownst to me, my thoughts alone were the reason for these difficulties.

In addition, reconnecting with my body had become quite natural. Rather than feeling helpless, I would merely think of moving my little finger, and presto! This decreased the time spent in paralysis significantly. However, I still found discomfort in the sensations that accompany feeling paralyzed. The difficulty in breathing and the fading physical awareness almost felt as if I were dying. Don't misunderstand me, it is not painful in any way, just very discomforting. The paralysis state, I believe, is like experiencing death in a small dose, sort of a mini-death. In a way, it is the halting of one existence and the beginning of another. And isn't that what death really is?

In the beginning, the sensation of consciousness teetering on the edge of unconsciousness almost always triggered my fight or flee instinct. And once that happened, I often aborted my attempts at an out-of-body experience and returned to the waking world as fast as I could. More recently, I have received letters from readers who've shared that they often felt nausea, which caused them to fight their way back to the waking state. And still others have complained of a heavy, nonphysical force pushing them down through the bed. This has been dubbed the "heavies" or the "haints" by some. And in my family these strange sensations were attributed to witches riding us as punishment for wrong deeds!

October 23, 1993

I went to bed about ten-thirty. At two-thirty I got up, used the bathroom, and went back to bed. I sang "Hu" softly for a minute and relaxed.

My mind wandered until a musical tone quickly brought me to full awareness. The tone was not from any instrument I've ever heard. It was indescribable. I felt motion. I was floating upward, then I could see the entire room. I looked around to see if anyone or anything was in the room with me, but there was nothing. I was both relieved and disappointed at the same time.

I thought about going up to the roof. As I went up through the ceiling, I thought of my body lying there in the bed. Suddenly I was back in my body with a bad case of the "vibes." I didn't want to stay there. I turned my attention to floating upward. Shortly, I was on a collision course with the ceiling again.

The thought of visiting my friend Kim came to me. With that, I started to move toward the bedroom window. I was halfway through the glass when the thought of my body reentered my mind. Within the blink of an eye, I was back in my body, fully reconnected (able to move).

I was determined to get out again, so I attempted to disconnect once more. The next thing I knew I was driving my car. Perplexed by the sudden shift in location, I asked myself over and over again, "Is this a dream?"

I recalled Dr. H. explaining that sometimes people create vehicles to move about in during an out-of-body experience. After reexamining the situation, I thought of leaving the car while it was still moving. Whoops! Bad idea! I still wasn't a hundred percent convinced I was having an out-of-body experience; this might be really happening. On the astral plane things that are self-generated appear to be as real as in the physical realm. I changed my mind and pulled the car over to the curb. For an astral vehicle the car was very responsive—easy to park too!

Without opening the door, I pushed through it and stood there next to the vehicle. As I turned my attention from it, the car became increasingly transparent and finally ceased to be. I stood there astonished.

I looked at my hands. They had an eerie glow around them. My entire astral body seemed to possess a soft luminescent quality.

I looked at my surroundings and, observing a nearby street corner, I asked to meet my guide there. I then flew to the corner, but nothing appeared.

I asked to meet the Mahanta, the Eckankar spiritual leader. I had been told by an Eckist that the Mahanta was capable of soul traveling at will. Members also told me if I wanted to see the Mahanta during soul travel, all I had to do was call him. Strike two! It's a good thing I was so apprehensive about meeting spirits. Otherwise I would have been disappointed.

A thought of my friend Kim surfaced again. In response I was drawn up to the second floor of a nearby apartment building. I entered a kitchen through one of the walls. I looked around for a minute or two, feeling like a cat burglar casing the joint. This made me uneasy, and I decided to make my exit through a window in one of the back bedrooms. It didn't occur to me that the apartment I was in might have been Kim's. For some reason that completely slipped my mind.

I dove out the window, turned left, and flew up an alleyway. I decided to experiment with speed and altitude. I noticed that I was able to exercise better control over these two elements.

I thought of going back to my body and rapidly returned. At first I thought I'd reconnected, but I realized I had not.

I was suspended, halfway in and halfway out, looking around the room for what seemed like a couple of minutes before I reconnected. I then raised my head and looked at the clock. It was 5:37 A.M. I had been traveling for over three hours.

I had read that most dreams last only a few seconds or minutes, usually not hours. This was one of the first indications this was more than a dream. Later I would find out two important things. The first is when I travel out-of-body on the physical plane, I seem to operate within the laws of time and space. But traveling at a higher vibratory level there is no time! By this I mean I have had experiences above the astral that seemed like hours, but when I returned and reconnected with my body, only a few minutes had passed.

A week later, I thought about the apartment and how I arrived there by merely focusing my thoughts. I began to wonder if that was really Kim's apartment. I contacted her and described the apartment to her with as much detail as I could remember. To my surprise, the apartment I described matched hers perfectly, even to a bedroom overlooking the alleyway. Later she sent me a floor plan of her place, and at once I knew I had been there.

Not only was I rapidly becoming a believer in the out-of-body phenomenon, but I was becoming increasingly interested in interacting with spirits on this plane. Yet this was a back-and-forth process. On some nights, like the one three weeks later, they still unnerved me.

November 10, 1993

I was dreaming when I became lucid to the extent that I was immediately back in my body and very much aware of feeling paralyzed. I felt two hands pulling on my hips, as if someone was trying to help me get out of my body.

I projected mentally, "Stop it!" In that instant I reconnected.

All of this grabbing, touching, and pulling was a bit too much. Was still another entity trying to get me to "come out and play"? I could not help but wonder about its motives. Later I would find that "its" motives were far beyond what I could ever have imagined. I think back to these earlier experiences, and I am still amazed. To think that entities, beings, apparitions, angels, or whatever they're called, could actually touch me. But the thing that would amaze me even further is that I could touch them as well. I can't begin to describe what it is like to be hugged by an angelic spirit. It has brought me peace beyond anything I've ever known.

November 14, 1993

I went to bed and, using the interrupted sleep technique, set the alarm for two-thirty. I got up when the alarm went off, stayed up for a short while, then went back to bed. I started to sing "Hu" softly. I lay there for some time, but nothing happened. Frustrated, I turned over on my side and fell asleep.

Suddenly I snapped to full consciousness: I was now floating above my bed. I decided to fly straight up through the roof. Who needs a door? As the upper part of my astral form penetrated the ceiling, I could see wooden ceiling beams and electrical wiring, then six inches of fiberglass insulation.

When I pushed through the shingled roofing, I found myself looking at an early morning sky filled with tiny stars. In awe I floated there above the roof of my house. I decided to try something a little different this time. Hovering there in the cool morning air, I projected, "I want to see the Light!" This Light that everyone in metaphysical circles alluded to, as I understood it, has been described as an angel, Jesus, even God.

Maybe I got too cocky, because I was abruptly gripped with unexplainable fear. I felt panic setting in; I cried out for Rosanna, my friend from the IANDS meetings. She had told me that two people having simultaneous out-of-body experiences could locate each other with very little difficulty.

Suddenly, I was moving very rapidly and stopped just as abruptly. I found myself standing in an apartment that was unfamiliar to me. Then all at once, without any warning, a rare thing happened. I lost consciousness. I remember nothing after that point. I woke up that morning still shaken from the unexplainable fear.

What I asked myself later was: Could the apartment have been Rosanna's? Did I get in over my head? Was I too high, too fast, too soon? In any case, I knew that I needed to develop more confidence before I attempted to see the Light. After I made my request to see the Light, I felt emotionally and spiritually naked. I felt as if all that I am, and have been, suddenly came to the forefront. I felt I should have been coming from a position of humility rather than one of arrogance. For some reason I not only knew I was not ready to see the Light, but at my present state of awareness, I wouldn't be able to handle it if I did.

 November 21, 1993

I sang "Hu" softly. I soon slipped into the state of paralysis, accompanied by the now-familiar buzzing sound. I felt the upper half of my body begin to float upward.

My astral vision came on-line, although I was not quite ready to look directly at the humanoid shape standing on my right about three feet away. This time instead of panicking, I concentrated on the thought that this could be my guide. I gathered all of the courage I had and said, "Hello." No response.

I repeated my greeting; still no answer. I was beginning to feel a little frightened, having been given the cold shoulder. I gave up my attempts to communicate, reentered, and reconnected. I watched the figure slowly disappear as I completed the reconnection with my body.

February 15, 1994

A strange mingling of planes occurred this time. I dropped off to sleep with my legs intertwined with my wife's. I was jolted to full awareness by two sets of arms pulling on my astral arms. I also felt a great amount of pressure near my tailbone.

I mentally projected that I didn't like that feeling, and the pressure immediately decreased but did not cease. I then reached up to feel the arms and hands pulling me.

The arms were soft and feminine. I reconnected and

opened my eyes. My wife said I had moaned aloud so she shook me with her legs.

Through this I learned that it is possible to have an out-of-body experience even though a human is physically touching me. However, Dr. H. said that touching makes it difficult to have an out-of-body experience.

Because of an unknown fear, I feel more at ease attempting an out-of-body experience when my wife is near rather than when I am alone. Is there safety in numbers on the astral plane? Sometimes I wish she could leave her body too. But since that is not the case, her physical presence is better than nothing at all. However, on the next rather brief excursion I was on my own.

February 21, 1994

My wife was on a business trip, so I went to bed alone. Attempting an out-of-body experience without my wife close by made me feel a little uneasy. I guess in a lot of ways I have grown astrally dependent on her. When the situation gets out of control, with her help I punch out. What's more, not all of my out-of-body experiences have been planned; some have just happened. I wasn't sure if I was prepared for this possibility. I decided not to try any preparatory techniques.

I drifted into a light sleep, and shortly, I woke up feeling paralyzed. Since I was alone, I was very reluctant to "get out." That's when I noticed that three to four humanoid figures were standing around me. They appeared to have hoods and robes. I wasn't quite ready for this (as if I ever am!). I fought my way back to the physical and reconnected.

Who were the new apparitions? They resembled religious monks. I wondered if I was simply dreaming or was this an authentic visitation. And if so, what could they possibly want from me?

In retrospect, the strange part about this visitation was that I was not the only one to see these hooded figures; so did someone else who at the time I had not met, but would soon become one of my dearest friends. Kimberly Clark Sharp, author of *After the Light*, wrote about the monklike entities long before we'd ever met. However, a major difference between her encounter and mine was that the figures also spoke to her: she saw them after her near-death experience and I saw them while partially out-of-body.

Later, I would discover that in fact the nonphysical entities I had seen *were* trying to communicate with me, but I was too preoccupied with suppressing my fear. This kept me from raising my own vibratory level to that of the hooded figures—almost like partially tuning into a television station where you can pick up the video but not the audio. This was also one of my first encounters with what I later found out are guiding spirits. These spirits come and go depending on the needs of the one being guided. In a way, they were preparing me for the role of a slightly different sort of guide, a psychic rescuer.

3

PSYCHIC RESCUE

Behold, I send an angel before thee, to keep thee in the way, and to bring thee unto the place which I have prepared.

—Exodus 23:20–21

March 14, 1994

I was dreaming that I was walking through my house when I became lucid within the dream. I was instantly back in my body, feeling paralyzed, except that in my third eye there was a picture. I focused on it, and it grew larger. Then I was in the picture. I leaned forward and took off into the sky. I flew around for a while, then returned to my body. The picture in the third eye reoccurred and I flew again, but this time while flying, I felt drawn to a large one-story building.

I floated through the front doors into a huge dining

hall. The room was filled with humanoid figures dressed in nineteenth-century attire. I immediately thought of *Gone With the Wind* and smiled, because I never liked that movie. Milling through the crowded room were three entities serving food and drinks. Although the room was filled to capacity, I somehow sensed these three shapes as the only genuine apparitions.

Feeling less threatened by one, a female entity, I cautiously approached her. She was dressed like the kitchen help from a Southern plantation. The female looked at me, then quickly turned back to her duties. At first I pretended to talk to the figures at nearby tables because I wasn't sure what was going on. Were these three figures entities or not? Why did I sense a difference between them and the rest of the figures? Why was I drawn here in the first place? Why did I feel the need to help them?

I watched the female entity for a while, then asked, "What are you doing?"

"Get back ta work!" she yelled, then moved away.

I approached her again and said, "You don't have to cater to these people anymore. They aren't real!"

"If'n you don't git back ta servin', you goan git whooped!"

I wondered for a moment who was going to administer this "whoopin'." I looked over at the two male apparitions, who glanced fearfully at me, then doubled their serving speed. I told the woman that I was leaving and that they were all welcome to come with me.

"We cain't do dat cuz they'll come after us!" blurted one of the males.

I turned to the seemingly crowded room and announced, "I'm leaving, and no one here's going to stop me!" (Where did all this courage come from?) The crowd of imitation people showed as much interest as a room full of mannequins. I walked to the front doors, went outside, and was immediately followed by all three of the entities I had been talking to.

"What we goan do now?" inquired the female.

"It's simple!" I said. "I will teach you how to fly!"

The four of us then headed down the street. One of the males kept looking back over his shoulder as if he expected an angry mob to burst suddenly from the building. Trying to ease his concerns, I turned to him and smiled. He seemed to sense my confidence and relaxed a bit. I instructed all of them to join hands, lean forward, and push off. We all flew! I kept low at first, then we began to climb rapidly.

I glanced back and forth, checking on my students' progress. Suddenly without warning they disappeared. After this encounter I was filled with questions. Where did the entities disappear to? Why didn't I fear them as I usually did? How long had these three been stuck in this . . . pseudoreality? I remember Dr. H. explaining that when people die, they sometimes become prisoners in their own self-created belief systems. For example, an individual may pass on and not know it, or refuse to accept his own death; then he may continue to "haunt" an old stomping ground, castle, hotel, etc.

It would later be explained by someone very close to me that not only should I have helped, but I was obligated to do so. "As you have been assisted, so shall you assist." I was told that it is part of a universal law that not only is practiced on the "other side," but was intended to be practiced on "this side" as well.

I became curious about the origin of the expression "the witches are riding you," used by my grandmother's generation to describe the paralysis. My aunt informed me she had a book that described witches traveling out-of-body. She told me that while she was reading the book, she became so frightened she tossed the book up into the top of her closet and tried to forget it. The book remained there unopened for years.

To make a long story short, I got my hands on this mystical manuscript, entitled *The Magic of Witchcraft*. The book describes how witches were linked with the dead and astral travel and how they communicated with spirits while out-of-body. The book also explains how witches lingered around graveyards to assist the newly departed dead to adapt to the spirit realm.

It appears that witches have long taken on the responsibility of rescuing lost souls. Was this what I had done? Could I be considered a witch? I began to wonder if this is how the paralysis became associated with "riding witches." Was it merely a coincidence that witches also practiced astral travel?

Three hundred years ago would I have been accused of practicing witchcraft? Were early astral travelers burned at the stake in Salem for speaking of their out-of-body explorations? An interesting connection is that this theory of "psychic rescue" is described in the book *Seth*

Speaks, by Jane Roberts, and in Robert Monroe's last book, *Ultimate Journey*.

This then explains the compelling urge I had to help the Southern plantation entities. Is this what I am supposed to be doing as part of my out-of-body travels? Am I destined to help lost and confused souls?

I began to wonder if this could now explain my fear of ghosts and spirits. Have they been trying to contact me unbeknownst to my everyday self?

April 5, 1994

That night I went to bed asking aloud for help in having a conscious out-of-body experience. I lay flat on my back and drifted off into a light sleep.

I woke up in the grip of the paralysis. I also observed that my wife was holding my hand; at least I thought it was her. I noticed the hand felt smaller than usual, almost childlike. This was frightening. I felt my astral body floating upward from the waist down. I projected, "I don't want to have an out-of-body experience."

A male voice spoke into my left ear and I tried to calm down. In response, the voice changed to female, as if it sensed my fear. The female voice was more calming but not much. As if to further ease my anxiety, the voice changed to a soft whisper. I found this less threatening, and I tried to relax. But I still didn't want an out-of-body experience, soft voice or not!

This conflict continued for a long time. I would force

myself to reconnect with my physical body, only to start drifting out again. Finally I reconnected and sat up. My wife was over on the other side of our king-size bed. Her back and hands were out of my reach. So whose hand had I been holding? To find out, I lay down and swiftly slipped back into the paralysis. The hand was there again, gently holding mine.

After I forced another earthly reconnection, I got out of bed, walked into the bathroom, and said aloud, "That is enough. I have to go to work in the morning."

Looking at the clock, I was alarmed to see it was one A.M. The whole series of events had taken three hours! I went back to bed and slept the remainder of the night without further interruption.

I had reached a stage when I was frequently contacting spirits on the astral plane. Yet the instinctive fear I felt kept holding me back. I did take a step forward on my next flight, but conquering the fear would continue to be my biggest obstacle.

April 12, 1994

I lay down and went through the usual preparations. I let go of the physical. I don't remember leaving my body, but I do recall the sensation of flying. I seemed to be on autopilot, flying high and steady.

I remembered I had spoken to an Eckankar friend about my failed attempts to meet my guide. My friend asked simply, "Did you look behind you?" I decided to take advantage of the autopilot condition, and looked back over my shoulder, toward the back of my legs.

To my surprise there was an "entity" supporting my legs and feet, helping me to fly! I waved at it, and it waved back. This was weird! It released my legs, flew up beside me, and hugged my waist. Fear closed in on me, but I managed to suppress it. The entity pointed downward at what looked like Stonehenge. We circled repeatedly over this ancient ceremonial circle. I could see figures moving in and around the huge stones. Each would stop briefly at a pillar, then move on to the next.

The scene reminded me, oddly, of patrons at an art gallery. The entity/guide began to tell me something about this famous attraction. I was concentrating so hard on controlling my fear that I missed what the entity said. At last I felt I'd had enough of this new experience and thought of returning to my body. I sensed a quick visual shift, then rapid motion. I was back and reconnected, yet I was left very disturbed by what I'd just seen!

The following week would bring another encounter with the same spirit. The same problem with communication would persist, though. I simply could not get past being mortally afraid.

April 19, 1994

I prepared for takeoff, relaxed, and let go of my physical body. I found myself flying in autopilot mode again. I looked over my shoulder, and sure enough, there was my autopilot. This time "Otto" (as in "Otto-matic pilot") did not wait for me to acknowledge his presence. Otto flew up and hugged me around my waist. I didn't want to look at Otto directly, but I did notice his color and skin pattern kept changing.

Once again Otto pointed down. As before, we were flying over Stonehenge. Fear crept over me as Otto spoke into my ear. I still cannot recall what Otto said. We flew round and round over Stonehenge. Otto continued to speak, and I continued to be very uneasy.

I decided to return. I thought of my body, there was a quick shift, I reconnected, and sat up. Although I tried, I was not able to go back to sleep this time. Until that point every out-of-body experience I'd experienced was unique; there had been no repeat trips. Two astral excursions to the same place must mean something, but what? What was Otto trying to tell me? No matter how hard I tried to remember, I couldn't. Soon I would discover that the information I received directly from Otto would be like planting a seed in the soil of my psyche for sprouting and blooming at a later date. I felt as if I was being spiritually cultivated.

I began to suffer from overconfidence, and I told my wife not to bother pulling me back to safety the next time. How foolhardy this was I found out several weeks later.

May 5, 1994

This night I let the feeling of the paralysis creep over me, forcing gravity to release its hold. I was suddenly aware of a loud roaring sound all around me. It was as if a windstorm was raging in my bedroom. The noise was almost too much to bear.

My floating motion upward came to an abrupt halt. As if from nowhere, someone or something pressed firmly up against my backside, from the back of my head to the heels of my feet. I projected mentally, "Otto, I don't like this!" No response. "Who are you?" I inquired, but still there was no response. I reached back with my astral hands and felt down a pair of arms until I reached the hands. I grabbed them and shook them, trying to provoke a reaction, to no avail. The hands felt lifeless and rubbery. The hands and fingers were oddly flattened and tucked in close to the legs.

This "thing" not only was pressing hard against me, it was breathing slowly in my ear, and I didn't like it. If this thing was Otto, then he was showing far too much affection for me. Fear sparked to life within me, and I hit the panic button. Abort . . . abort . . . abort!

Nothing happened! Where was my wife? Hadn't she heard me? Then I remembered telling her if she heard me moan, don't touch me, because I can reconnect . . . all by myself. I panicked completely, forgetting about the "little finger" trick. I moaned again, with no response. I felt a hard shove, reconnected with my body, and sprang to a sitting position.

"Didn't you hear me!" I exclaimed.

"You said you could handle it by yourself!" my wife mocked, then turned over and went back to sleep.

I got up and walked into the bathroom, still shaken. Yet when I looked into the mirror, I realized what had transpired during the out-of-body experience. The "thing" had been my own body! I remembered tucking my hands in close to my thighs as part of my preflight preparations. And the slow deep breathing made sense for a sleeping body.

I went back to bed feeling a little foolish. Being afraid of my own body was one reason; the other was the overconfidence that my wife pointed out for me.

I was still mulling over this lesson when a new manifestation of astral travel showed itself to me. I had been thinking in terms of my astral body being a copy of my physical body, but a new journey showed me yet another fascinating variation.

May 10, 1994

I lay down that night not really thinking about an out-of-body experience. I relaxed and drifted off to sleep.

I woke at the sound of an intermittent loud crackling. I was vibrating like crazy! I prepared for liftoff, focused my thoughts, and rose majestically upward into the . . . ceiling fan! I stopped and quickly looked back down.

On the bed lay two figures; was one of them me? Until

this journey I had avoided looking directly at my body. I'm not really sure why, but I looked this time, briefly.

My wife was on her left side with her back toward my body. It was strange how detached I felt looking at what was supposed to be me. Yet it wasn't really me at all, more like a costume I wear. I moved over to a corner and quickly scanned the room, looking for uninvited guests. I saw no one, but something was different. No, *I* was different. I was not using my astral body. I was not using any body at all!

I can describe this in no other way but this: I appeared to be a pinpoint of consciousness and no more. I could see the room in all directions at once. Where was my astral body? Did I forget it somewhere? I was overwhelmed, amazed, and ready to return. I floated back to my body without incident and reconnected.

What was this all about? I seemed to have left my astral body behind. I began to wonder why I needed an astral body in the first place.

Could it be that the shock of not having a pseudoastral body would be too disorienting? Did a part of me, maybe the higher self, create the vehicle to provide some stability for me? During this experience I also became aware of vibrational levels that I could not perceive on earlier jaunts. Without the limitations of the astral body, I was somehow now able to sense other nonphysical levels expanding all around me. All of this was starting to make sense to me somehow. The astral body is just that, a vehicle for the astral plane. But in order to transition beyond this first level, I would need to shed yet another outer shell.

A further strange connection occurred a few days later. Over the past few months I had developed a hunger for metaphysical literature. I read everything I could find. The odd thing was, most of the books I read were gifts or were recommended by a friend, or sometimes by a complete stranger.

For example, on one occasion, after eating breakfast at a local restaurant and waiting at the cash register to pay my tab, a man commented about the book I was holding.

"That's a good book," he said. It was *Seth Speaks* by Jane Roberts.

"I know," I said. "I can't seem to put it down."

He asked, "Have you read *Visions*?"

"No, I haven't," I said.

"Get it!" He smiled and walked out.

Yet the book referral that produced an odd psychic connection came while I was attending a monthly IANDS meeting with Dr. H. At the good doctor's insistence, I recounted a recent out-of-body experience. After I finished speaking, one of the IANDS members walked up to me and slipped a piece of paper into my shirt pocket. He said, "This is your next book!"

I looked at the paper: *Zolar's Encyclopedia of Ancient and Forbidden Knowledge*. The next day I ordered the book. Soon I received a phone call from the bookstore in Newport Beach. *Zolar* had arrived and I could pick it up. I drove to the bookstore, bought the book, and left. I walked through the parking lot toward my car carrying the book, thoroughly wrapped in brown paper. When I tore off the paper, I was shocked by the cover—it featured a picture of Stonehenge. Remembering my last two trips, I began to feel a weird tingling sensation creeping up my spine. What the heck was this about?

Even though in the last two out-of-body experiences my guide had been there without my seeking him out, I found out this is not always the case. I guess he has better things to do than baby-sit an apprentice astral traveler. But I tried to contact him anyway.

August 20, 1994

After I used the interrupted sleep technique, I performed an abbreviated preflight routine and teetered on the edge of sleep. Still in my physical body I snapped to full lucidity, having been startled by the sound of a roaring wind.

While still in the grip of paralysis, I decided to choose a destination before I left my body. Flying near the clouds would be interesting. I faded or dissolved out of my body and materialized flying high above the ground. That was a different way to start! I paused, then reached for the sky, and climbed at an incredible rate of speed. Soon I was among the clouds. Most were heavily saturated with moisture. I was homing in on a large, dark cloud when my internal warning system went off. A peculiar feeling of danger took hold of me, which confused me. But one thing was clear, change course, now!

Suddenly there were no clouds, just an endless night filled with tiny points of light. All around me were twinkling stars. It was beautiful.

The moon seemed to be rushing toward me. I veered off and turned back toward the Earth. I could see oceans and land masses through a cloudy veil.

I kept asking myself, Why haven't I done this before? The land soon was rapidly approaching. Down, down, down . . . I was falling! I screeched to a halt high above the ground. I paused, assuring myself I was still in control. I dove downward again, aiming toward the west coastline of North America.

As I approached the coast of California, I could see the faint lines of highways and roads. Soon I could see cities and clumps of buildings. I flew in low over a street. People were crossing streets or standing at bus stops. I flew up to a street sign and floated there, staring at the sign. I could not read the words. I could see letters or symbols but could not make it out. I felt astrally dyslexic.

I decided to perform a quick shift to simplify returning. I focused my thoughts on my body, felt a shift from location to location, reconnected, and opened my physical eyes.

This journey left me in awe and wonderment. Not only had my suspicions been confirmed about not being of this earth because I was more than capable of leaving it, I now began to think that truly we are of the stars. This is fitting, as the word *astral* means exactly that. While I was far beyond the environment needed to support my corporeal counterpart, I felt I could journey light-years into the void of space, fueled only by the power of thought.

In early September 1994, I had an interesting short out-of-body experience that harked back to my sense of being a psychic rescuer. After lying down and performing a quicker relaxation routine that night, I drifted off to sleep.

Dreaming . . . dreaming . . . slight awareness . . . I could hear a voice . . . I snapped to full lucid consciousness. I was in a crowd of forty or fifty nonphysical beings. Confused and disoriented, I asked myself, "Is this a dream?" This crowd of entities were all focused on a single being toward the front and slightly above everyone else. No one paid any attention to me. I was just part of the spiritual audience.

The "speaker" said all beings present were a part of a particular purpose. I couldn't control my emotions and became overly excited. Was I in a class for astral travelers? Were these beings disembodied spirits, or were they like me, spiritual tourists? A wave of excitement overpowered me, and I could feel myself being forced to return to my body. I released and gave in. I immediately returned and sat up in bed, astonished at this new encounter with otherworldly spirits.

September 20, 1994

Several weeks later, I went to bed at 9:15 and dropped off immediately. I woke up at 1:28 to use the bathroom. Back in bed, I couldn't fall asleep. I tossed and turned until 4:12, when finally something began to happen. My body slowly fell asleep, and the sense of being paralyzed took over.

My legs began to rise upward. I wanted to sit up, and I did. Doing this felt so natural that I had to make sure I was sitting up physically. Experimenting, I stood up—and noticed my feet were touching the carpet. I walked over to the foot of the bed. As I walked, I simply thought about floating, and I did.

I thought about walking on the carpet, and I floated down and walked. I caught sight of the mirror on the back of the bedroom door, and noticed I had no reflection, like Count Dracula.

I put my hand through the mirror on the back of the bedroom door, paused, then dove through it into the hallway. I floated there, trying to decide where I should go. Kim came to mind, and I focused on her. Without warning I felt two hands on either side of me gently grabbing my arms. The hands turned me around and pushed/pulled me out through the wall. I saw nothing but blackness. Then I found myself standing in front of an apartment building. I was totally disoriented. Confused, I forgot my destination. I decided to call for Otto again. I pointed to a spot ten feet away and said, "Please appear over there." I looked behind me, but no Otto. I then began to think of my body, experienced a quick visual shift, felt a slight bit of movement, and reconnected.

For some reason my memory fails me in the astral body, and I sometimes forget where I am going.

Processing thought appears to be quite different during soul traveling, almost as if a link with the brain has been interrupted. It appears that people, places, and things with which I have no emotional ties are of little significance.

For example, if I planned, while in the physical state, to soul travel to a foreign country to observe top secret activities, this event would likely not occur. Not because I am incapable of doing it, but for the reason that it has no spiritual significance. While soul traveling, I wonder if I think more like the spiritual being that I am rather than the earthly personality self I've slipped free of.

January 14, 1995

For some reason I had trouble falling asleep and tossed and turned until long after midnight. Finally something started to happen, even though falling asleep was initially my goal.

The presence of the paralysis was heralded by a swarm of buzzing bees. Astrally I sprang to the sitting position and looked casually around the bedroom. I focused on floating and rose a foot or so above the blankets. I became aware of the sound of water coming from the other side of the bedroom door. I began to recognize the splashing sound; it was the shower in the bathroom.

I wondered why my wife had decided to take a shower in the middle of the night. As I focused on the sound, the door and wall, which separate our bedroom from the hallway, abruptly ceased to be a visual obstacle. I could see the bathroom door framed by the light within, which was physically impossible.

My attention shifted slightly, and I became aware of a humanoid figure lying in the bed next to my body. Oh, my God! I thought. If my wife is in the bathroom taking a shower, then what is this resting beside me?

I began probing the figure with a part of my consciousness. I was amazed at what transpired because I was not using my astral hands to identify this reclining intruder, I was using pure thought. I could mentally touch this being from head to toe all at the same time.

Who is this? Fear crept over me. I bolted toward my body, using the abort sequence, the little finger trick, and fright. I reconnected at the same moment I felt a familiar elbow.

"Are you okay?" my wife asked.

"Uh, yes . . . I'm fine," I replied realizing the blatant error in observation I had just made. My wife was not taking a shower, my older son was. Feeling foolish, I lay down, listening to the sounds of my son Brandon completing his shower and turning off the water.

The next morning I asked Brandon why he had decided to take a shower at two o'clock in the morning. "Dad, I didn't get off work until one-thirty this morning," he said. "Sorry, did I wake you up?"

"No, I was already awake, sort of."

This experience was a major clue for me about the properties of the physical world. As humans, most of us are aware of nothing beyond what our five senses tell us. But to a nonphysical spirit or soul traveler, the physical plane is something to perceive only if one chooses to do so. So, if I can look past the physical world just by focusing my thoughts, then how real can it be or how important can it be? Is it just an illusion our five senses have convinced us of? Have we all agreed the physical plane exists in order for it to continue as a learning environment for souls? As Jesus said, "In my Father's house are many mansions." I suggest the physical world is just one of these mansions we can see, but it is far less influential in our lives than the mansions we can't see.

4

A CHANGE IN PERSPECTIVE

When lost in the mental jungles of confusion and fear, realize that God knows the way out!

—Joseph Murphy

The effect the out-of-body experiences and metaphysical literature has had on me has been lasting. Even as early as April 1993, shortly after I started, several impressions became a permanent part of my consciousness.

The first is that I no longer have a fear of death. I never dwelled on it before, but death lost its sense of finality. I believe there is a hereafter, and whatever defines me as me will consciously survive. My relationship with IANDS and Rosanna has strengthened this belief tremendously. I have heard numerous firsthand accounts of near-death experiences and to me they appear to be akin to my journeys. However, I have not died! And, unlike what I have heard about the near-death experience, I seem to have more control over my travels. Most of the time I can choose where to go and when to return. I also have what I describe as a "knowing" that has stayed with me since nearly the beginning. I am convinced that the lack of a physical body is my timeless natural state, and existing with a physical body is as temporary as a dream.

During that early out-of-body experience in April 1993 something happened that forever changed me. While I floated there above my body, all of a sudden I felt as if my consciousness was somehow opened up, and information about everything was abruptly poured in. For the first time in my life I had absolutely *no* questions about anything. For a fleeting period of time I felt that I knew everything. Suddenly the ups and downs of the earth life system made sense. All the mysteries, frustrations, disappointments, and miracles, all had a distinct purpose. I didn't know it at the time, but later I would be told that I may have had what metaphysicians refer to as a kundalini experience. And while I was in the midst of this phenomenon I had the overwhelming feeling of finally being home. Not in a physical state, but in a consciousness state. This I refer to as *soul consciousness*. One of the primary lasting by-products of this soul consciousness is losing the fear of death and realizing that although I am on this earth, I am not of it. Moreover, I and we are incredible and powerful spiritual beings having a human experience, and not just humans having a limited spiritual experience.

My current relationships with everyone around me—close relatives, friends, and strangers—are more open, honest, and caring—unlike anything I've previously thought probable. My wife and friends have repeatedly referred to me as "a spiritual guide." I take this as a great compliment, although I don't agree. I do know I have shared my insights into problems or self-defeating behavior with others, and that seems to have helped them.

Sometimes my suggestion consists of a different way of looking at a situation. The strangest part about the insights is I have no idea where the information comes from. In most cases the guidance I've offered is news to me too! I do not make predictions or anything of that sort, just observations that appear to be very clear to me.

On several occasions I have applied the new insights to my own life with positive results. This remains an enigma . . . at least to me.

I was invited by my friend Kim to explore my imagination in a slightly different manner. Kim invited me to attend a past-life-regression experiment conducted by a prominent hypnotherapist in Newport Beach, California.

My relationship with Kim is a little unusual. She feels almost like a sister. This I find strange, because I have no siblings and have never wished for any. But there is a bond that has been apparent to me from our initial meeting. Still, when I drove to Newport Beach, I kept asking myself, "Why are you doing this? This is a waste of time and money. Turn around while you still can! What does this have to do with out-of-body experiences anyway?"

When we arrived, Kim explained how she'd done this before with remarkable results. We walked to a nearby house, knocked on the door, and a middle-aged woman opened it and greeted us with a smile.

"Welcome! I'm Dr. Carbone," she said, turning for us to follow. "We are just about to get started." She grinned as we climbed the staircase.

We entered a small but cozy den where six other people were already seated. We exchanged greetings, then found our chairs. Kim and I were seated on opposite ends of the room. I felt a little silly and sat there staring at Kim.

Dr. Carbone explained to us what was to come and said we should relax and follow her instructions.

The doctor started a tape of prerecorded music and began to lead us toward a light hypnotic state. I relaxed my body with relative ease, almost like preparing for a soul journey. After ensuring that the participants were thoroughly relaxed, Dr. Carbone began to describe a forest with tall, swaying trees. In the forest she described a long, winding path and directed us to follow it. At the end of the path was a house—one that we had lived in during a past life.

I have a pretty active imagination, so I gave in to her prompting and made an effort to visualize this abode. In my mind's eye grew an image of a white and brown German cottage with darker brown shutters. Following her guidance, I moved to the door, opened it, and walked in. I could see a half-circular staircase on the left and a dining area toward the right.

I moved to the dining table and observed neatly placed pewter dishes. I was intrigued by this because Dr. Carbone stopped verbally directing us after I entered the doorway. I noticed a warm, flickering glow radiating from the fireplace. I turned and walked over to the staircase. I climbed quickly and entered one of the bedrooms at the top of the stairs. Inside on the left wall was a closet that stood out from the wall and was supported by short wooden legs. I opened the closet and found it filled with women's clothes. Then a strange feeling swept over me. I had an instinctive impression that the clothes were . . . mine! This was getting too weird.

Dr. Carbone cut in, "You are leaving that life through a long tunnel. As you emerge on the other side, you will be in a life previous to the one we just visited."

I found myself standing on a snow-covered mountainside, studded with tall trees. Smoke from nearby campfires permeated the air. But I sensed something else. People were moaning. No, people were dying. No, *my* people were dying. *We* were starving. I looked down at my feet, which were shod in furry, knee-high, crudely crafted boots.

This was too much! I looked up from my boots to see some of the dead being carried away on two parallel poles, drawn by horses. Then it suddenly hit me. My people were dying because the cavalry had driven us away from our homeland and into the mountains.

"I want you to go to the last day of that life," Dr. Cabone interjected.

Suddenly I was lying down, covered by thick furs. I

had been mortally wounded during a one-sided battle. We had returned to fight for our land—the land of our fathers. We didn't have a chance and were brutally slaughtered.

I looked around. I was in a circular, pointed room with a fire burning in the center. A flap of hide at the top was partially open to let the rising smoke escape.

"At the count of five, I want you to return to this life," Dr. Carbone interrupted. "You are healthy and whole."

"One . . . two . . . three . . . four . . ." I sat up slowly, thinking, "What a great imagination I have." Like the dead coming back to life, the other time travelers began to stretch and yawn.

Dr. Carbone looked straight at me. "So, tell us about your experience. Did anything happen?"

"Uh, no. I was just using my imagination." (Wasn't I?)

"Please, don't be shy. Tell us!" insisted Dr. Carbone.

Reluctantly I shared my story, but only included bits and pieces with very few details. While I spoke, I couldn't help but notice Kim staring at me with a blank look and her mouth wide open. "What's with her?" I thought. I didn't think my story was that interesting.

I quickly ended my tale and relinquished the podium. The good doctor thanked me for sharing, then began prompting the next person. I noticed that Kim was still staring at me. Had I made a fool of myself? Before long the doctor asked Kim about her experiences. Kim's stare finally broke off.

Kim began to tell the exact same story as mine. While I listened, I felt very disappointed in her. Why would she blatantly copy my *imaginary* story? Was she trying to give my story some validity, to keep me from regretting this entire venture?

As she described the table settings inside the cottage, then the radiant fire and the large wooden dining table, I thought, Wait a minute! I hadn't shared that part of the story. Was this just a lucky guess? No, the details were far too elaborate.

Kim then began to describe her reincarnated life after the German one. She pictured the snow scene in the mountains, but from a slightly different perspective. She told of the starvation, the dead being dragged off on two poles.

Hold on a minute! I'd completely left that part out! My mouth dropped open. Now it was my turn to stare at her. Kim continued to describe events and details that I had imagined but not shared. I was at a loss.

After the session ended, Kim and I continued to compare our experiences. We were both shocked. "I don't believe in reincarnation!" I said. "At least I thought I didn't!"

Was there some logical explanation? *How could we share the same . . . daydream?* Kim began to tell me how more times than not, souls somehow reincarnate together lifetime after lifetime. Well, I never would have guessed that I could leave my body and fly all over creation. Maybe reincarnation *is* possible.

Sometime later I would discover that like vibrational souls somehow reincarnate with each other over and over again. I now believe that Kim and I, for some reason, fit into this category. Are we here to assist each other through this school of life? Thinking back, I see that Kim has helped steer me into more than a few opportunities for spiritual growth, and I hope I have done the same for her.

5

A RELATIVE ENCOUNTER

Life is a state of becoming, and death is merely a part of the process.

—Jane Roberts

During one of my out-of-body flights in mid-1994 I was drawn to a location I can only describe as "a meeting place." I do not believe this place is a physical location. If it is, it's not on Earth. At least twice I have felt an irresistible urge to "blink out" and follow its magnetic pull. When in this location I felt overwhelmed by the countless entities seemingly milling around. These beings paid very little if any attention to me.

I wondered if this was an entity's self-created pseudo-reality, or was I in the midst of hundreds of entities? Oddly, I felt only a little fearful. I scanned the crowd and was puzzled as to why they were here, wherever *here* was. Suddenly, I recognized the face of a being a short distance away—looking directly at me! I thought, "No way; it couldn't be her." The entity bore a striking resemblance to my late aunt Vera. Why would I see her? I haven't thought of her in years. I almost never think of her.

Aunt Vera was my mother's sister who died of cancer in August 1982. I was very close to her in my youth, but we had grown distant during most of my adult life.

Now here was my aunt, standing/floating directly in front of me. I felt fear rear its ugly head. If this is her, I thought, then she is the first spirit whom I knew and who lived and died in my lifetime. I was a pallbearer at her funeral. This encounter unleashed a flood of emotions that I could not handle. I thought of my body and retreated for home at warp speed. When I reconnected, I was dazed by what had occurred.

Should I tell my mother I saw her deceased youngest sister? Was it really her? She did appear to recognize me, while the other beings paid no attention.

A few days later, I slipped free of my body and took off on a local sortie. Soon I experienced that magnetic pull again, and I followed it. I arrived and found the multitudes the same as before. This time I had one person on my mind, my aunt. As if responding to a page, there, a short distance away, appeared Aunt Vera. This time she slowly approached me.

With two parts courage and one part fear, I curiously inquired, "Aunt Vera, aren't you dead?"

"Yes, I am!" she said, smiling at me.

I stared at her, perplexed. Yes, it was her—a part of me knew it. I also could feel an intense sensation of love emanating from her.

I felt a need to return to my body, focused my thoughts, and sped off. After reconnecting, I reflected on what had occurred and realized the ever-present fear of spirits had diminished dramatically. Through Aunt Vera, I understood a little more about them somehow and was comforted.

This strange current running among families was illustrated in a more dramatic way in early October 1994. At this time my wife and I had been following her uncle's progress after surviving surgery that removed a grapefruit-sized tumor from his chest. My wife's uncle was now in critical condition in a Los Angeles hospital. On October 7, at 10:15 P.M., the phone rang once. My wife answered. By the sound of her voice, I knew the inevitable had happened. Her uncle was free from suffering at last.

I comforted my wife the best I could, until she drifted off to sleep. As I relaxed beside her, I wondered if it was too soon to attempt an encounter with her uncle. Was it even possible? I decided to try and focused my thoughts on him as much as I could. I did the preparatory techniques, relaxed, and released.

Shortly thereafter I was aware of the detachment that signals the presence of the paralysis. I allowed the upper half of my astral body to rise slightly above the physical one. Just then I felt the approach of a presence beyond the bedroom door. The presence was strong and unmistakable; someone was definitely approaching.

I stared as a humanoid figure stood motionless in the doorway of our bedroom. I could hardly control myself. Was my wife's uncle paying us a visit, or was it . . . a burglar?

I instantly reconnected and sat up physically. The doorway was vacant. I lay back down, willing myself to return to the paralysis, and quickly I did. I rose above my corporeal body again—and the apparition appeared partway through the doorway.

Was this my wife's uncle? And if it wasn't, then who else could it be? I could not make out the facial features. Even if I could, I might not have recognized him because I'd only met him a couple of times. But, seemingly at my request, his spirit was paying us a visit.

The entity slowly backed away from the doorway, and I no longer felt its presence. I reconnected, sat up, and reached for my journal.

The encounters with my aunt and my wife's uncle reminded me of an incident twenty years earlier. Then I considered what happened to be coincidence, as so many people do. In light of these astral meetings, though, I've decided that this phenomenon represented a glimmering of a much wider universe open to us.

On March 15, 1973, I was an Airman First Class in the United States Air Force, stationed in Wichita Falls, Texas. That day a few fellow servicemen and I decided to spend our free time at Six Flags Over Texas, an amusement park.

We all boarded the largest roller coaster and prepared for the worst. About halfway through the ride, though, a feeling unlike anything I've ever felt consumed me. Overwhelming sadness and depression dominated me totally. I could no longer enjoy the remainder of the ride. When I exited the coaster, my friends became immediately aware of my mood.

"Are you okay, Al? You don't look so good."

"I'm all right, but something is very wrong. Something has happened, I can feel it!" I said.

It didn't make sense. I was supposed to be having a good time, not depressing everyone. But the feeling that gripped me was not to be ignored.

"I have to call my mother in Los Angeles," I blurted out. I found a public phone and called home. My mother answered, and without pausing to say hello, I desperately inquired, "Mom, what's wrong?"

She replied, "Albert, we have been trying to contact you most of the day. Your father just died."

It was as if a subconscious part of me sensed a problem, and the conscious part of me knew where to find the answer. The overpowering sadness that I felt made sense now. I shared the sad news with my friends.

"That was weird, Al! How did you know?"

"I have no idea," I replied. "No idea."

Later that day, I returned to the place where I was living just outside of Sheppard Air Force Base. As we pulled up, I noticed a note flapping back and forth on the windshield of my car. It was from the Red Cross, stating that it was urgent and that I should contact them at once. I called the number on the note, sure of its purpose.

After arriving back in Los Angeles, I found out more

about my father's passing. Although repeatedly warned by his physician, my father died from alcoholism. He drank himself to death.

Now in July 1994, after having experienced what was becoming a series of supernatural encounters, I decided to explore the world of ghosts. In the following two years I attended numerous lectures and classes on esoteric subjects such as mind projection, psychokinetic energy (spoon bending), opening your "third eye," lucid dreaming, and ghost hunting. The majority of these were held at the Learning Light Foundation in Anaheim.

After attending these classes, I signed up to get the monthly newsletter. In a few months I received an edition that featured an internationally known psychic and medium. Rose Clifford was said to have acquired, at the age of sixteen, the capability to communicate with the spirit world. She was now fifty-two years young. In the days before my own soul travel, I would have scoffed at mediums or psychics, but the recent encounters had changed all that.

I made an appointment to see this medium. Because of her popularity, I had to schedule it two weeks in advance. During that time I kept telling myself I was not going to tell the medium anything that might give her an opportunity to mumble vague, if true, things about me.

The medium greeted me with a starched British accent. She motioned for me to sit facing her, then asked to hold my wedding ring. Saying nothing at all, I smiled and handed my ring to her.

The medium considered for several minutes, then

stated, "There is a man here, a tall man." (Okay, that's pretty generic.)

"You were his boy," she relayed. (This was beginning to sound a little rehearsed.)

"He says he is sorry he left you." (Well, I guess I wasted my time and money!)

"Oh, this man drank a bit, didn't he?" (I began to listen more, but still gave no response.)

"As a matter of fact, his drinking is what killed him." (She had my full attention, although she did not specifically say it was my father.)

"There is also a grandfather here. He appears to have had a drinking problem too." (This was true about my mother's father, but it was still too ambiguous.)

"That's very interesting," I finally said.

"I also sense that you are being influenced by or have been in contact with one or two beings of light," she asserted.

The medium said she saw me speaking at a podium before a large crowd of people. I did not know it then, but two months later I would be asked to speak at a popular men's club to a group of a hundred or more. Although I tried to decline the offer, the scheduled speaker developed a severe throat infection, which left me without a way out. During the entire one-hour lecture, I kept thinking back to Ms. Clifford's prophesy.

Who would have thought that a misunderstood occurrence like night paralysis would have changed my life so profoundly. "The witches are riding you!" is how my grandmother had described it.

In all my excitement about out-of-body experiences, I completely forgot that my mother still suffered with the feeling of paralysis. I wondered if she, too, at the age of seventy-two, could have an astral experience. If nothing else, I could relieve her concerns about what happened to Robert . . . couldn't I? Did my mother's fear of the witches prevent her from "getting out"? One day I sat with my mother and shared some of my discoveries about the paralysis.

Surprisingly enough, she was very receptive and eager to perform some of her own experiments. A week or two later she told me the following:

"I woke up paralyzed and nearly forced my way out of it," she said. "I then thought about what you said and relaxed a bit." She then repeated several times, "I want to float upward." She told me that she began to rise, and as she did, she became aware of someone holding her hand. Unlike me, she was not fearful, even though this was her first flight. She did, however, feel uncomfortable outside of her body and quickly returned.

My cousin Robert had also suffered from feeling paralyzed, but he had died a few years earlier. I'd been told that he was in the paralysis state when he passed on. Catherine, Robert's wife, said her husband was moaning, which was their signal for her to shake him and wake him up. Normally, this was enough to rouse him, but Robert soon stopped moaning and slipped away.

In the later part of 1994, I spoke with Catherine. She explained to me that they had been married for thirty-two years, and Robert had had witches "riding" him for the entire time. All those years opportunity had been knocking on Robert's door, but he was afraid to answer. Catherine shared with me a story that I believe shows just how close he may have been.

One morning she woke early and left Robert still sleeping in their bed. Their granddaughter, Denise, was visiting and rose from bed early as well. Denise, eager to see if her grandfather was awake, walked into the bedroom and crept over to the bed. "Poppi," as she called him, was lying there with his eyes closed, repeatedly moaning. Thinking Robert was dreaming, she left without disturbing him. Catherine heard the barely audible moaning and looked away from the television to see Denise slipping out of the bedroom.

"What is that noise?" she asked the child.

"Oh, that's just Poppi making that noise," Denise said innocently.

Catherine realized that the moaning was Robert's signal to be shaken awake, ran into the bedroom, and shook Robert frantically. Robert woke and immediately complained.

"That child came into the room, looked into my face, and left without waking me!"

"She didn't know you wanted to be awakened," defended Catherine.

I find it interesting that Denise saw her grandfather lying there asleep, which implies that his eyes were closed. He spoke of her walking into the room, looking at him, then leaving. Could Robert have been peering at her through his third eye? How could he see Denise at all? Was he slightly "out-of-body"?

Catherine told me that not only did Robert have a problem with riding witches, but so did his father, his brother, and even their daughter.

"Your daughter?" I asked, interested.

"Yes, Catty still suffers from that problem," she replied.

I could hardly contain my excitement. There was someone else with whom I could share my discovery. I asked for Catty's address and phone number, thanked Catherine, and left.

Later that week I met with Catty, who was in her early fifties, and shared practically everything I could remember about my out-of-body experiences. With enthusiasm I told her that she, too, could soon be off on her own excursions. After listening to me for a half hour or so, she gazed at me with a rigid expression and remarked, "Why would I want to do that? I just want to know how to reconnect."

I was snatched back to reality. Just because out-of-body experiences had become a major part of my life, why would I assume they would be for her too? I shared with her the "little finger trick," apologized for taking up so much of her time, and left.

At first I thought that Catty's response represented the opinions of just a few, but sadly I have found many people who were unable to at least consider what I was sharing about out-of-body experiences. Once again fear acts like a roadblock to higher learning. Catty reacted as if there was no turning back if she ever decided to follow me. Which was far from the truth. But then maybe she's right, because I have come to the realization that there is no turning back for me, not that I'd want to turn back. Doing so at this point would be like trying to climb a tree that has been cut down long ago.

Finally, I'd like to relate a humorous journey—though intriguing in its possibilities. Those near and dear to you are not always people.

January 11, 1995

I fell asleep around ten-thirty, and woke up about one, feeling slight vibrations. I did some exercises and slipped into the paralysis.

With the help of my astral vision, I began to slowly scan the bedroom. Unexpectedly, outside the window I heard my dog, a German shepherd named Bear, barking frantically. Normally Bear sleeps inside the house at night, but evidently one of us forgot to let him in. Why was he barking right outside my bedroom window? In the seven years we'd had him, he had never done that. I reconnected with my body and sat up. Bear immediately stopped barking. I curiously parted the curtain and looked out of the window. I could see Bear calmly walking back from the other side of the backyard. I got out of bed, let him in, and went back to bed, grounded for the rest of the night.

Here's the question: Did Bear somehow know I was out-of-body? He stopped barking the moment I reconnected as if he knew, and started walking away from the window even before I looked out. Are animals sensitive to astral forms or the disembodied life force? Did Bear sense some type of energy field I was generating?

6

STAR LIGHT, STAR BRIGHT

With God all things are possible.

—Matthew 19:26

The astral body is a wondrous vehicle. It provides a sense of security and stability for the earthbound self by emulating the physical body. It allows us to appear well-dressed, beautiful, handsome, and as tall or short as our ego wants us to be. But the astral body is not always needed. I believe it is just one more costume we wear. It appears to serve the same purpose as a child's security blanket. This first became apparent to me the night I found myself only a pinpoint of consciousness, and this sensation would be repeated on Halloween night—of all times—the following year. Yet something even more wondrous would take place: I would find my higher self.

October 31, 1994

I meditated for twenty minutes before I fell asleep with my hand on my wife's leg. Shortly thereafter I was yanked back to full awareness, very much conscious of feeling paralyzed. I sat up astrally and surveyed the bedroom—no third party. I moved to my left toward my wife in a backward sliding motion. I was dragging something behind me that felt like a deflated inner tube.

At that moment I realized that parts of me were in three separate locations. My physical body was flat on its back on the right side of our bed. My astral body was the deflated inner tube dragging behind me, and *I* was a pinpoint of consciousness. I surveyed all of this in bewilderment.

As I continued to move around my wife's head, I discovered to my amazement that I was not my normal size. I was tiny and my wife appeared to be a giant. I had slid to her left side, staring at her with childlike curiosity, when she suddenly moved. As if I were at the end of a leash, I was instantly jerked back into my bodies. I reconnected and realized that my physical hand was still resting on my wife's leg. Every time she moved, so would my hand. This had forced me to return.

I lay back, trying not to move, and mentally reached out for the paralysis. I detached from the physical and sat up astrally.

I found Otto standing on my right toward the foot of the bed. I smiled and greeted him openly without fear. Otto floated over to the side of the bed and stopped near my pillow. I stared at him with wonderment. I couldn't help but notice the luminescent brilliance of my spiritual friend. The warm angelical glow that emanated from him was awe inspiring. Then, without warning, I received mental information that obliterated the last remnants of my religious upbringing.

I want to share what I now believe to be an inescapable self-realization. My guide, my guardian angel, my Otto-matic pilot, I believe is my *higher self*. It stretches far beyond my imagination to fabricate a concept like this one. But I believe the being is *me* in a higher form of consciousness. An inner part of me somehow understood that this "Oversoul," as Jane Roberts referred to it, has been with me from my physical beginning. In essence, he has always been with me, and always will be.

Abruptly, inadvertently, I reconnected; my wife had moved again. I moved physically away from her and attempted to return to the state of paralysis, to no avail. Moving physically had somehow disrupted the continuity of the out-of-body experience. I lay there completely connected and awake.

In retrospect, I thought, I now know that I am not alone, I will not be alone, nor have I ever been alone! I believe that I am guided by my higher self, which in turn is guided by "All That Is," God.

This view was seconded at a recent IANDS meeting, when a newcomer, sharing her experience for the first time, spoke of an expression that her angel/guide said to her that left her puzzled. Toward the end of her near-death experience, just before she returned to her body, her spiritual guide shared this insight: "The smaller light follows the larger, and the larger light follows the *Source.*" To me, the meaning of this statement was very apparent.

November 7, 1994

I fell asleep early, about nine, and woke at one. I tossed and turned until three-thirty (the interrupted sleep technique, sort of!). I lay there, mentally reaching out for the paralysis, until it slowly crept over me like a river of warm honey. I focused on picking a destination and casually thought of walking in our den. Just like that I ceased to be in my body in our bedroom and materialized in the den.

This "blinking out" at one location and "blinking in" at another threw me off guard. I paused and asked myself, "Am I dreaming?" My gaze panned the room as I started to walk through the house. I floated up about five inches and skipped through one of the bedrooms to my four-year-old son's bedroom door. I paused, walked through the door, and slid over to my son, Devon's, bed. I noticed that he had kicked off the blankets I had so carefully tucked in. I began to hover over his bed, feeling protective of this frail little being.

I left my son's bedroom through the wall, performed a quick patrol of the rest of the house, then casually thought of my body. As if I were on an invisible conveyor belt, I headed toward my bedroom. Reconnection was so slightly noticeable I wasn't sure if it had happened or not. The little finger trick placed me back in control of my body.

These seemingly endless variables are amazing. I seem to be able to fly to a location or "blink out" and "blink in" to wherever my thoughts are focused. What are we that we can do these wondrous things?

During this out-of-body experience I also found that my emotions seemed to be greatly intensified, almost as if I had become the emotion itself. For example, the feeling of love for my son was greatly intensified as I hovered over his bed. Many sages have spoken of love as a source of great light, and this night I felt I had discovered what they meant.

November 11, 1994

I became aware of the paralysis but was not fully focused on the feeling of falling backward or the shortness of breath that sometimes accompanies it. Before I could file my mental flight plan, I blinked out of my physical body with no destination in mind. I knew immediately that I was not at the controls and that something was amiss.

I blinked into the middle of nowhere. All around me there was an endless darkness, except directly in front of me, there was a single source of bright light. It was as if a blue-white star was burning a hole in the middle of a black velvet curtain.

The Light radiated outward in long bright rays, like a crystal comprised of thousands of needlelike spears. The shards penetrated my very soul. I can best describe this experience from the perspective of the reentry heat shield on the Apollo 11 space capsule: As the space capsule's heat shield resisted the extreme temperatures of an Earth reentry, microscopic pieces were vaporized and burned away. The Light pierced through me. Like the capsule's heat shield, parts of *me* were burned away. Parts I no longer needed. The Light was excruciatingly wonderful. All at once I was wrenched from the Light and tossed back into my body.

"Are you okay?" my wife asked.

"I'm all right," I said, wondering why I had come back so abruptly.

"You were moaning, so I shook you," she explained.

At this point, I tried not to focus on my swift return because I wanted desperately to go back. I didn't have long to wait. I was overcome by paralysis and blinked out. I blinked into the same locale as before, to the same radiant brilliance. And just as before, I felt the unwanted pieces of myself being burned away. Subconsciously this entire sequence of events was completely familiar and welcome.

Oh, what a heavenly Light!

Then, without warning, I was slammed back into my body, *hard*!

"Are you all right?" my wife asked.

"Yes, I'm fine!" I responded, feeling a little irritated. After this, try as I might, I was not able to return to the

Light. It seems that a feeling of anger is extremely pernicious to the chain of events leading to an out-of-body experience. Negative emotions are likely to stifle any attempts made to achieve a higher state of consciousness. In my physical life, I have begun to find out that anger is truly a useless tool. We use it knowingly and unknowingly to change persons or situations around us for the better. At least that is the intention. In truth, it is an instrument of control, dominance, and destruction. Reflecting back on my use of anger, I can't think of one time when it has made my situation better, not one! More times than not it made the situation worse. And if we have enough faith in God that everything is being guided anyway, why would we need anger to change it? Faith and anger don't mix.

November 17, 1994

I could barely stay awake. I read for a while, then fell asleep for the night, or so I thought. My wife woke at one-thirty, got up to check on Devon, then got back into bed with a thump.

I was now awake. I lay there feeling completely abandoned by the sandman. I tossed and turned until 3:20 A.M.—on a weeknight. The thought of driving to work semicomatose did not appeal to me.

"Well, Al, since you've practically performed the interrupted sleep technique, you may as well top it off with a preflight!" I thought to myself.

"Okay, I will!" I was ready to try anything at that point. I completed the preflight, disengaged my astral parking brake, and waited. After about ten minutes, I could feel paralysis creeping up on me. My ears were assaulted by a loud crackling. I focused my thoughts, heard a loud "pop," and was literally tossed out of my body.

As if I were being summoned, I headed straight for the wall that separates the living room from our bedroom. Without hesitation I dove through the wall and quickly came to a halt. I had emerged partially into a black empty void. The upper half of my astral self was in the void, and the lower half was still in my bedroom.

There was no sound, surface, or light source out there, just a nothingness that seemed to stretch in all directions. Although I could not see it, I sensed a barrier of some kind far, far ahead of me.

I ventured forward, only gradually increasing speed. After what seemed like an eternity, I came to a stop. "Turn around before you get lost," a fearful voice inside commanded.

I looked for a landmark, but the darkness was endless. I thought, "What if there's nothing on the other side?"

After checking to see if I'd changed my orientation, I mentally put myself into reverse and backed out the way I came in—feet first. I felt a surface behind me and backed right through it to my bedroom.

"Maybe you should try this direction some other time!"

I turned toward the bedroom door and floated into the hallway. I floated down to the carpet and walked into the living room to examine the wall I should have emerged from earlier. There was nothing peculiar about the wall on this side. I decided to perform a quick reconnaissance of the house.

I zipped though the kitchen and into the den. Observing nothing out of the ordinary, I turned and retraced my path. I turned the corner and headed toward the living room and almost ran right into Otto.

He seemed to have been waiting for me. Another entity stood a few feet away but did not approach us. No words were exchanged, just images and feelings. And all of this seemed very familiar to me. It was as if I had been interacting with the two of them, in this manner, for a very long time.

I sensed that the entity a few feet away was not there because of me but because of my wife. Could this be her guide or angel? What also occurred to me was that I felt no fear at all! I felt myself being recalled to my body. Without resisting, I quickly returned to the physical.

The famous line of Franklin D. Roosevelt, "We have nothing to fear but fear itself," applies to the soul traveler as well.

I wonder how many times a spirit has communicated with my soul unbeknownst to my earthbound self. Is this how these beings guide us during the course of our lives? And is this guidance normally on a subconscious level? I can't help but think about the many times I've suddenly remembered a dream that was somehow suppressed or forgotten. Could this be one of the hurdles we must leap if we are truly to progress spiritually?

7

BEAUTIFUL DREAMER

Dreams are the language of the soul, and because we dream every night, it is important we learn this language!

—Ruth Montgomery

Have you ever asked yourself why we dream? Everybody does it. One third of our lives is spent lying on our backs. During this state of seeming inactivity, the mind is actively at work. Some people believe that dreams are messages from the subconscious giving us clues to solve our everyday problems. Others believe there is no value in these late-night fantasies. I, too, believe dreams are clues to daily existence, but this is just the tip of the iceberg.

Why is it that during the dream state people have

reported a variety of incidents that seem to link this state of consciousness with the physical world? A woman once told me she had misplaced her car keys and was unable to locate them for several days. One night after searching frantically for them, she gave up and went to bed. After lying down, she once again thought of her misplaced keys and prayed for assistance before drifting off to sleep. Sometime during the night it came to her in a dream that her keys were resting inside a multicolored vase. Upon waking the next morning, she remembered the dream and recalled a similar vase in her living room. Leaping from the bed, she grabbed the vase and poured out its contents. There, to her surprise, were her missing keys.

There are numerous tales similar to this one. The Bible, for example, is riddled with tales of people's dreams where they are given insight and solutions to problems. I feel, however, that these types of events are not restricted to an individual's belief in them. In fact, these types of occurrences have transcended religion and have influenced the atheist as well.

So, what is going on? During my many experiments with altered states of consciousness, I have experienced a "knowing" that has been accessible upon leaving the body. However, I do not believe that one must travel outside of the body to tap into this energy source. This seemingly infinite source of energy has been described as a "universal consciousness" by prominent researchers like Dr. Joseph Murphy.

This universal consciousness, I believe, is the same

energy source that psychics and mediums somehow tap into. Residing in this level of consciousness is an inexhaustible amount of information.

Depending on an individual's perceptions, accessed information will manifest itself in symbols, images, feelings, and sometimes in an unexplainable "knowing." In other cases the receiver of the data may not be adept at interpreting this information and may require the assistance of a spiritual guide. If there is a significant desire or need for information, the guide may act as a conduit and convey this data to the receiver during a dream. However, I do not believe information extricated from this universal consciousness flows completely unrestricted; it depends on the individual's karmic requirements. I also do not believe our futures are predetermined or predestined.

Based on this premise, I believe our futures are only probable—in other words, what *might* happen as opposed to what *will* happen. Depending on the soul's spiritual needs, data received via the universal consciousness will either be denied or severely restricted. Perhaps a superior wisdom has imposed unalterable "safeguards" or data flow limitations that appear to work in *our own best interest.* The amount of data we can access may be governed by the impact it will have on our Earth life experience.

This brings me back to one of the more exciting types of nocturnal imaging, the *lucid* dream. This is defined in the dictionary as: "The state or quality of being aware that one is dreaming. Bright with the radiance of intellect; not darkened or confused; clear and distinct awareness."

In childhood and as a young adult I would continually "wake up in my dreams." This was how I described the feeling of being alert and aware. I would then fend off any monsters or creatures that had the misfortune of crossing my path.

Sometimes a nightmare would become so horrific it would force me to ask myself, "Is this a dream?" After this my mind would wake up while my body remained asleep. I was then capable of changing the plot of the dream. In short, I became both actor and director. If that meant I had to assume the identity of Superman, then so be it. All in all, there seemed to be very little I could not do as long as my thoughts remained focused.

The key to becoming lucid during a dream begins while you are still awake. While you are out going about your daily routines, periodically ask yourself, "Am I dreaming?" Practicing this exercise while awake may condition you to question your state of consciousness while dreaming. It works for me!

8

PLANES OF CONSCIOUSNESS

We fear the darkness only because we don't know what is there.

—Robert Monroe

In this chapter I'd like to share with the reader and future soul traveler some information about what it is like to explore multiple levels of consciousness, primarily the astral plane. As you may know, access to this information has been shrouded with secrecy since the beginning of time. The levels of consciousness as explained by Eckankar are: the physical, astral, causal, mental, and etheric planes. Information about these levels has been distorted by countless dogmatic teachings.

These levels of consciousness appear to be separated by thin areas of endless darkness, or a black void. Each level possesses its own signature vibration. The physical level vibrates at the lowest rate. In order to transition to higher levels, one must somehow change or increase the vibrations of the soul body. But this is true only above the astral plane. On the astral plane the soul occupies the astral body. The only way I have been able to ascend above the astral plane is to leave the astral body behind. And when the astral vehicle has been shed, a lighter, brighter, permanent nonphysical body can be realized. This remarkable light vehicle has often been referred to as the etheric body.

The vast majority of people are afraid to learn more about other levels of consciousness because of fearful condemnations like, "It is the work of the Devil!" In other cases individuals have been denied access to this ancient wisdom because they were deemed spiritually unqualified. In the past, knowledge of this sort could only be acquired by dedicating months or years of study in remotely isolated ashrams and/or monasteries.

For those future soul travelers it is important to acquire as much knowledge as possible, preferably before one sets sail into the world of what I like to call the "dear but not departed."

It is my aim to share some of this knowledge with the reader—hoping this will assist you in avoiding detours or roadblocks that will surely be encountered.

I find it extremely disheartening that due to religious dogma, Western culture has been left behind in the quest for spiritual enlightenment. Hindus and Buddhists of Eastern civilizations are generally farther along the path of spiritual advancement. The religions of the East readily accept their spiritual origins and continue to seek further spiritual guidance and awareness. The concept of reincarnation, for example, is not only accepted but encouraged and taught. However, in modern Western society, this concept is only in the embryonic stages of development. In spite of the widely accepted teachings of Edgar Cayce and the profound insights given by the entity Seth via Jane Roberts, this awareness remains obscure and virtually unexplored.

I'd like to provide some reassurance for those who are fearful and a partial road map for the more adventurous. You need not be fearful when delving into the many levels of consciousness, because they are a *natural* part of our existence.

It has not been easy for me to overcome my own unfounded fears. Deep within myself, I have found my fear to come from or be driven by a basic "fight or flee" survival instinct. As you probably know, without this survival instinct we would likely have gone the way of the dinosaur and become extinct. If early humans had not run screaming into their subterranean shelters or massed together to repel a ravenous predator, we would not have survived.

This basic survival instinct, however, is a hindrance in exploring the astral plane and beyond. You have to work to get past it.

The next thing to understand about the astral plane is that it is not devoid of life. The beings there are quite unlike anything you are familiar with, but don't kid yourself: They are very real. They can be quite different, though. The level of spiritual enlightenment achieved by these beings may vary a great deal. In addition, just because the life forms there qualify as spirits and will likely possess far greater capabilities than most of us, it does not mean that all are wise and forthright.

When a person has passed on to a higher level of consciousness, that person doesn't automatically become an angel, guide, or spirit master. I have found that we retain a great many characteristics of who we are in this life, both the positive and the negative.

This does not mean that these entities should be feared; it just means that not all encounters with them will necessarily be for your higher good. The astral plane, as you may know by now, is just one place we go when our bodies die.

However you end up there, be it death or soul travel, you may experience a variety of unexplainable sounds. The Eckists refer to these sounds as the voice of Sugmad or God. I myself have heard many different sounds during soul travel. Strangely enough, Eckankar has listed many of these sounds on a rather intricate chart. For instance, the sound associated with the astral plane is the roaring of the sea. The causal plane is the tinkling of bells. The mental plane is running water, and the etheric is buzzing bees.

A key point is that the astral plane may seem like a place to go, but in actuality it is something you become aware of. The astral plane, like oxygen, permeates the physical plane. On the astral plane we unconsciously create a "body double" comprised of astral material. This astral body, like the physical body, serves as a containment vehicle for the soul.

As I have mentioned earlier, it provides transitional stability for the newly dead as well as the soul traveler. Nevertheless, it is not permanent, nor is it absolutely needed. I have slipped out of it, leaving it behind like a worn-out pair of coveralls. If you manage to accomplish this, you will still retain all the simulated senses you have in the physical: sight, sound, touch, and in rare situations taste.

Now, there are many avenues to take while touring the astral plane; but all the while be advised that deceased loved ones and strangers may present themselves with little or no warning.

In the beginning keep your jaunts localized, gradually venturing farther as you gain more confidence. Remember, physical locations on this planet and beyond are merely a thought away. You can quickly get in over your head in the blink of an eye, so keep it short and simple.

I also want to point out that during the out-of-body experience the power of thought is a tool that must be handled carefully. Anything you can imagine you will see or experience. This alone indicates the awesome capabilities of our soul.

I have come to believe that thought is just as powerful in the physical as in the astral plane or beyond. After all, everything around you presently began as a thought in someone's mind; it just didn't manifest instantly as it would have on the astral plane.

For example, in early 1992 I was diagnosed with the

debilitating disease of multiple sclerosis, better known as MS. After suffering two devastating attacks, I was hospitalized with severe vision and equilibrium problems. My prognosis was not good. My doctor explained to me that my physical health would likely degrade over the next few years. Shortly after receiving this less than welcome news, I began to have consciously controlled out-of-body experiences. After all, what did I have to lose by trying this method of healing? To make a long story short, be it coincidence or not, at present I have no physical manifestations of this otherwise crippling disease.

Many years have passed since I was first diagnosed with MS. If I chose to believe that the doctors had the final word on my recovery, I most likely would be confined to a wheelchair. But they were wrong! I am healthy and whole today. I believe that had I chosen to follow my doctor's lead, my thoughts would have affected my body at a cellular level, thus manifesting the MS.

The belief in certain religious dogmas is important, but first I should clarify that I would never say what a person should or should not believe. We, as beings of light, have a "free will," and it is because of this freedom to choose that the soul is capable of spiritual learning and evolving.

For the would-be soul traveler, there may exist within you certain religious beliefs that will prevent you from transcending the astral. When you get past these constraints, you will be able to experience the multiple dimensions above the astral plane. No matter how painful it is, I have had to discard, and I continue to discard, antiquated beliefs that I held dear. You may find this painfully necessary when searching for your own ultimate truth.

I once read a book a friend recommended called *Ask Your Angels*. The basic premise is angels have wings. It also states that everyone has his/her own invisible wings. I wonder if this is a way of providing something for humans to relate to by merging tangible wings with unbelievable creatures such as angels. Does this make them easier to accept? The only concern I have with a prejudgment of this sort is this: A person who is unfamiliar with the creative magic that is always present on the astral plane may impose his own visual images onto another being. This will likely contaminate the journey and prevent the traveler from having a dogma-free experience.

I won't pretend that I have seen every type of nonphysical entity that may exist, but none that I saw had wings. *I* fly without wings. I would think that the angels do too!

9

THE ULTIMATE TRUTH

Before I formed thee in the belly, I knew thee; and before thou camest forth out of the womb, I sanctified thee.

—Jeremiah 1:5

Before we delve into the mystery of the ultimate truth, perhaps we should first ask the ultimate question. For me that is: Why are we here? I will not pretend that I have found the answer, but I will offer a viewpoint influenced by my soul travels.

First of all, we exist independently of our physical bodies, hence the ability to travel out of the body. For me this has been proof enough that I will survive death's embrace. Second, we must accept that a multitude of beings exist in a dimension other than the physical.

Third, it has been well documented that during hypnosis and after a near-death experience, hundreds of people have reported experiencing a detailed review of their lives. How many times have we heard the expression, "My life flashed before my eyes!" This phrase has always been associated with life-threatening circumstances. At this point I must query why would a review of past indiscretions be of value after departing from the world of the living? If we die and go to heaven, hell, or somewhere in between, of what possible benefit is a review of what is now unchangeable? Could it be we are given this life review in order to learn by our mistakes, in hopes of not repeating them? I suggest that this may be one of our first clues that we somehow return to the Earth life system. And if so, then what is to be gained by returning to experience another life? Could it be to facilitate spiritual evolution of the soul?

I have personally come to believe that life without reincarnation is like a stage play with only one act. There just isn't enough time for character development.

So, providing we do somehow return to the physical and live again, where will all these life lessons eventually lead us? Is there some distant yet attainable goal? Based on my spiritual travels, I would say yes, beyond a shadow of a doubt!

On the physical plane you are born, grow older, and finally experience death. It is then that some of those experiencing near-death report being drawn into a tunnel filled with swirling multicolored lights. Some report no lights at all, just an eerie blackness (which sounds similar to the black void I've experienced). When they arrive at the end of this tunnel, many recall being met by a deceased relative or one or more beings of light. This generally occurs on the astral plane. According to the *Tibetan Book of the Dead,* this location or state of consciousness is referred to as the "bardo."

I have mentioned earlier that in April 1993 I experienced an overwhelming feeling of finally coming home. Only after myriad repeat visits have I come to accept this state of consciousness as the bardo. Since then I continue to have a deep longing for what I now know to be home. This longing has become a permanent part of my waking consciousness. I am constantly homesick! So be advised, you too may develop this agonizing longing for home.

Sometime after exiting the tunnel, a life review must be endured. I say endured because looking back at one's own life has been described as a mixture of pleasure and devastating sadness. The extent of sadness usually depends on how kind or cruel a person has been to others. Those experiencing near-death have described feeling the exact same pain, sadness, and hurt they thoughtlessly and selfishly caused another.

After the life review, a soul now has the opportunity to plan the next step on its own evolutionary path.

On the next page is a chart depicting the various arcs of spiritual evolution. There are probably a multitude of evolutionary paths an individual soul may follow or choose, but for the sake of simplicity, I have limited this illustration to these five paths.

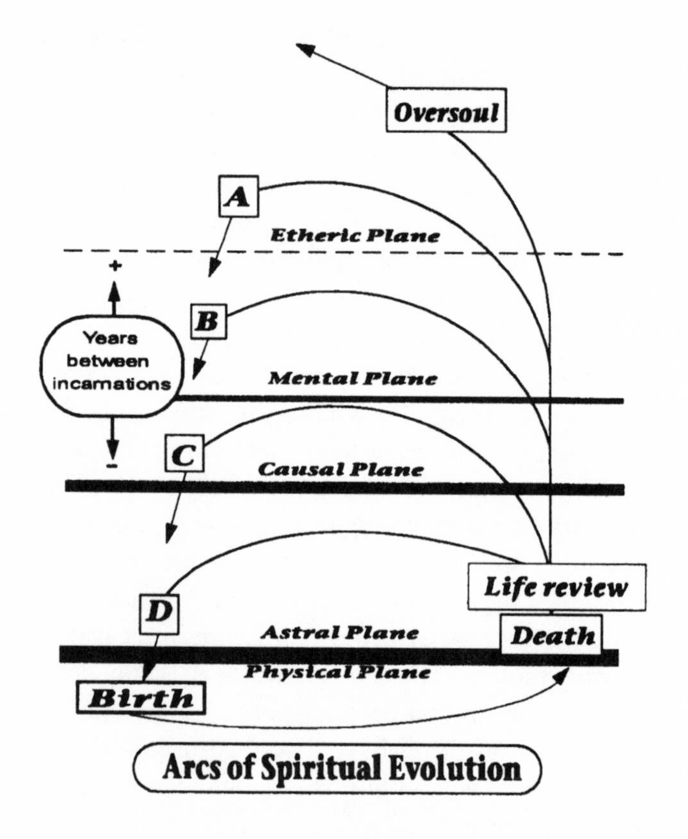

Arcs of Spiritual Evolution

On the chart the D arc represents a type of soul often referred to as earthbound. This type of soul has also been affectionately nicknamed a "repeater." This is because the type D must reincarnate numerous times to gain a minimal amount of enlightenment. These souls ignore essential insights given during the life review and often fail to satisfy inescapable karmic requirements.

The type D soul is likely to reincarnate quickly, missing the benefits of more careful planning. The type D soul has also been blamed for a vast amount of the world's heartaches and sorrows. This type of soul is usually narcissistic and self-destructive.

Arcs C and B depict a soul at a higher state of evolution. This type of soul is deeply affected by the life review and usually is remorseful when confronted with past transgressions. These souls will generally direct more energy toward preparation and planning for the next life. At the C and B stages of evolution, the time spent in the bardo increases, allowing for higher arcs into the upper levels of consciousness. These souls are just becoming aware of who and what they truly are.

The type A soul is a highly developed being and has attained a very high level of self-awareness during its physical incarnation. While living on the physical plane, these souls are usually spiritual teachers, masters, or shamans. The type A soul often has a profound impact on the human population as a whole. These enlightened souls may very well be messengers from God. Some of them have been variously labeled a saint, a master, a guide, or prophet. The primary focus of this type of entity is to lead lost souls back to All That Is, or God.

Last, but not least, is the Oversoul entity, a being of unimaginable capabilities and possibilities. This type of self-aware consciousness is virtually unlimited. This being is no longer tied to the seemingly endless cycle of reincarnation. The Oversoul entity has been referred to as a god in the making. An Oversoul is a being that has progressed light-years from the type A soul. The Oversoul is rapidly progressing toward the ultimate truth, which is to become a coworker and cocreator with God. I believe this is the irrevocable destiny of the soul. This brings to mind the expression, "We are all created in God's image." After slipping free of my astral body and existing as a pinpoint of consciousness, being created in God's own image continues to possess possibilities far beyond these earthly vehicles of flesh and bone.

10

PREFLIGHT PREPARATIONS

√ *When we realize our thoughts create our future experiences, then looking within ourselves for happiness becomes our only recourse.*

—Unknown

If you have read this far, then you must be asking yourself, "How can I do that?" When I asked what percentage of people actually achieved a controlled, conscious out-of-body experience, I was told about twenty to thirty-five percent. I'm not trying to discourage anyone. I just want to suggest that a trial of patience may be in store for you.

These techniques are not guaranteed, of course. They are just some examples of what I've tried with a certain amount of success. Try them all until you feel comfortable or achieve some results. If you fall asleep, don't be concerned, because you may be closer than you think.

If you feel more comfortable surrounding yourself with white light, then do so. If you like to use crystals, then use them. The goal is to get as relaxed as possible. One other thing you must remember, prior to traveling and during soul travel, is that you are a being of light and nothing can harm you unless you think it can. Even then, after the experience you will emerge unblemished.

I have found that my worst enemy during out-of-body experiences is my own uncontrolled imagination. I have learned that whatever I imagine—devils, demons, or pink elephants—will be created instantly. I have found that it is important to keep my thoughts clear and uncluttered.

In addition, it is important not to prejudge or guess what is going to happen, because you might be the one creating it! Keep dreamlike manifestations from contaminating your out-of-body experiences. But controlled use of the imagination during a journey can be quite amazing and downright fun.

I offer the following techniques and mental exercises with the hope that they will serve you as they have me.

The Paralysis State

Find a warm, comfortable, quiet place to perform any of the following exercises. Once you have started, do not move under any circumstance—not even to scratch your nose!

Let's first examine in more detail the sensations before, during, and after the paralysis. There is a good chance that you may already be experiencing some sort of night paralysis.

As the paralysis begins to creep over you, a feeling of falling backward may accompany it. This sensation may cause you to react by catching or stopping yourself. Yet this might break the chain of events and abort your disconnection from the physical. You may also feel as if you cannot breathe properly, but this will quickly pass. If you get through these barriers, you may become aware of a variety of sounds at a deafening volume—sounds such as buzzing, roaring wind, electrical sizzling, crackling, and even a musical tone or instrument. Don't try to identify the sounds at all. You will be at that mysterious place where dreams are born. Keep your thoughts clear or you might be confronted by your own creation, two heads and all!

Later, as you develop more control, you may want to experiment by creating a dream to experience. This will likely take a lot of practice. If you reach this stage, you may hear *voices* or see *shapes* and *images*. At first, treat them only as distractions. You may also become aware of a floating or upward movement. This sometimes occurs without asking. If you are not rising skyward, try repeating the command to do so. Remember, there is nothing to fear but your own fearful, uncontrolled imagination. You cannot be injured or killed. However, be advised you can feel pain if you believe you have been injured by something or someone. In addition, you need not worry about returning to your body, because the slightest thought of this will make it so. You also do not have to worry about someone taking over control of your body. Divine Power has given it to you, and you alone. So let go and enjoy!

Full Relaxation Routine

Lie flat on your back with your arms at your sides and close your eyes. This is called the earth position. Make sure that your head is not propped up with extra pillows; one is usually sufficient. Starting at your feet, tighten the muscles in your toes and feet. Hold for ten to fifteen seconds, then allow the tension to melt down into the mattress or floor. Repeat this for your other leg muscles, ankles, calves, thighs, etc. Continue this process until you reach your face; don't forget your neck and shoulder muscles. Tighten and relax your jaw, cheeks, and forehead. Now tighten your hand into a clenched fist and hold it. Slowly begin to tighten the forearm and upper arm (biceps and triceps). When you've done this, hold your entire arm rigid for approximately twenty seconds. Release, and allow all the tension to melt away. Slowly scan your body, mentally looking for any tension that you may have missed. If necessary, repeat the tighten and release procedure.

Now lie there breathing normally and repeat in your mind, "I want to float upward." Be patient. It may take a lot of practice, and in the beginning you may just drift off to sleep. Try not to become frustrated or tense; you will just be defeating yourself. So relax!

The Taylor Preflight

Lie flat on your back in the earth position. Take in a deep breath and hold for approximately four seconds, then release the breath through slightly parted lips, as you sing "Hu." Try using a low vibrating tone while you exhale slowly. You may need to first practice the Hu to find a tone level you feel comfortable with. If you are worried about disturbing your mate, you can sing Hu very softly.

Mentally begin relaxing your muscles, starting at your feet. Move through each set of muscles similar to the full relaxation routine, but relax them only. Do not tighten your muscles this time. Breathe normally and think about floating or rising upward. Remember, be patient.

Abbreviated Preflight

Assume the earth position, close your eyes, and get comfortable. Imagine a three-foot ball of warm glowing energy suspended two feet above you. Breathe in deeply and rhythmically, but not forcefully. As you inhale, mentally pull a stream of energy down from the ball. Go down and through the bottom of your feet up into your lungs. When you exhale, push the energy up and out the top of your head, back into the ball of energy above you. As the energy enters your feet and legs, feel the relaxing warmth it brings. Let this warmth flow through your entire body as you become part of the energy circle. Mentally release control of your arms and legs; they are no longer a part of you. Relax and listen for an inner signal (buzzing, crackling, zipping, roaring wind, or sparks of light). Again, be patient. You may just fall asleep.

Preprogramming

This technique may seem easy, but sometimes the simplest things work the best. Go to bed as you normally do. Then repeat aloud, "I want to have an out-of-body experience!" Or spell aloud several times the phrase "astral travel," A-S-T-R-A-L T-R-A-V-E-L. Pronounce every letter two or three times, then let go of all your thoughts (easier said than done). Repeat this three or four times if you need to do so.

Interrupted Sleep Technique (IST)

This exercise can be used alone or combined with any of the other techniques. As I have described earlier in this book, you go to sleep about nine o'clock and set the alarm for one, then get out of bed. It will not be effective if you wake up and go right back to sleep, so get out of bed! Stay up until three-thirty, lie flat on your back, and relax. I usually chant "Hu" or use a breathing technique that is similar.

Focus on an Object

This routine is very difficult to master. The first few times I tried it, I ended up falling asleep. Lie down and perform a breathing routine that suits you. Ten minutes is usually sufficient. Stay flat on your back and relax. In your mind's eye, picture a simple object like a square or triangle. Remember to keep it simple. A square or triangle will be difficult enough to focus on without your thoughts drifting off somewhere. If your thoughts do drift away from your primary focus, gently bring them back to your chosen image. You will quickly find out that the mind loves to wander. You will also find out that with a certain amount of practice, you should begin to hold your images longer and longer.

This can be a very frustrating technique, so make sure you do not get flustered, because if you do you will only be defeating yourself.

Find Yourself

Lie flat on your back and perform one of the preflight routines you feel comfortable with. Ask yourself, "Where is my consciousness located in this body?" You are a pinpoint of consciousness. Where are you located? Are you deep within your chest? Are you in the center of your brain near what is called the pineal gland? I picture myself about two or three inches behind my eyes. Look there!

As you search for yourself, casually relinquish control of your arms and legs, as if they were no longer a part of you. Tell yourself you no longer have the desire to feel them. Repeat this step for the upper and lower torso.

This will narrow down the area you have left to look for your consciousness. At this point you may feel a vibration or shaking. You may feel yourself falling backward through the mattress. Don't fight it. You may also feel as if you are having breathing problems. If you didn't have breathing problems before you started, this may be a sign of the paralysis. You might be at the point of disconnection from the physical. The previous sensations have been some of my largest hurdles, mainly because the feelings can be unpleasant and trigger a fight-or-flight instinct. So don't panic. Those of you who reach this disconnection point will soon get used to it. If nothing has happened, yet you feel disconnected, you may need to focus on floating upward. Just repeat two or three times, "I want to float upward."

The spiritual path that I have taken has sometimes been a bumpy one, but I now know that every emotional twist and turn has brought me to this point. I have found that emotions like stress, anger, envy, or negative thoughts hamper if not sever the chain of events leading up to an out-of-body experience. So, get rid of them. (Piece of cake, right?) Approach this type of experience with as much inner peace as possible. This is something that can't be faked; you must be steadfast in achieving this state.

Anger, hate, and envy will point you in the opposite direction of inner peace. I have found that in the majority of contentious situations, the outcome had very little long-term negative impact on my life. But the associated tension has had a profound impact on my out-of-body experiences.

I have switched to acquiescing in personal disputes, rather than holding stubbornly to my own point of view. Sometimes we defend our correctness to the brink of insanity. Remember, inner peace is the goal, and that peace should reflect in as many areas of your life as possible.

I don't believe that stress, tension, or any other emotion can be extinguished by merely throwing a mental switch. The effects or remnants of negative emotions may require thorough housekeeping deep within, even though there are few visible indications on the surface. This negativity may be at work on a subconscious level, preventing you from achieving total relaxation. In other words, you won't be going anywhere!

I often wonder why we must prove we are right, and someone else wrong?

Why must there always be a superior and a subordinate?

Why must we constantly jockey for a position of authority?

Why must we strive to establish a pecking order, when none is needed?

Why must we be one up or one down?

I am not suggesting that in situations where you may have concerns for your own or someone's safety you should not stick to your convictions. However, when the stress of being incorrect is far less than the stress of proving correctness, why choose the latter—especially if neither outcome has a long-term effect on your life?

One more reason why we shouldn't hold such inflexible views is that we don't all think the same way.

It frequently appears as if we all create and operate in simultaneous yet slightly different realities. For instance, two people can be exposed to the same situation yet perceive and recall the event differently.

My personal rules for life are simply stated by this basic credo, which helps me to balance my existence, in the body and *out.*

Judge, and you shall be judged.
Hate, and you shall be hated.
Lie, and you shall be lied to.
Cheat, and you shall be cheated.
Curse, and you shall be cursed,
but Love, and so shall you be.

If all people would adhere to this simple yet challenging guidance, no doubt we'd all be charting a steady course toward spiritual enlightenment. I believe that whatever you put into your experiences is ultimately what you'll get out of them.

There appear to be two dominant emotions we take with us when we leave this world, love and fear. The latter pushes us farther away from All That Is, and the former speaks for itself. God and love are synonymous. Remember, how we relate to one another has a profound physical and spiritual impact on all of us as a whole. And I believe we will ultimately have to account for this.

Our everyday thoughts are all too often generated by the things we fear—for example, fear of being alone, penniless, homeless, jobless, and loveless, just to name a few. These fears have a profound effect on the actions and decisions each of us must choose in the course of our everyday lives. It is because of these fears that we either spring into action when none is needed, or fail to take action when we know we should.

We seem constantly to be afraid of what *might* happen! And what might happen is always bad. We allow our behavior to be controlled by this fear instead of being led by our higher selves. Ironically, because of this fear the vast majority of us haven't the slightest clue that there is a higher self. Thus, fear becomes an impenetrable curtain between the personality self and the God within. So, simply put, fear is for people who don't know God. If you arrive at this realization, you will have very little difficulty during your own soul travels.

To all of you who've shared your kind words with me in your letters over the past two years, I say simply this, thank you from the bottom of my heart and soul. You are exactly who I wrote this book for. And for those of you who've had near-death or out-of-body experiences, please remember this: Yes, you did get a glimpse of what it is like to go home. And how fortunate we are to know beyond a shadow of a doubt that there is no death, only a change of worlds.

Through my journeys, a part of me has discovered it will not only survive death, but will instead finally wake up from the restricted awareness of life. But I do understand that while in these corporeal vehicles of flesh and bone, the mind and body instincts are extremely strong and influential. And because of fear we will all slip backward from time to time. For a lot of reasons, this is why we are here, because we must all strive every day to master our emotions.

I pray that through our earthly experiences we all will somehow learn to put the spiritual horse back in front of the cart. We must try to let our spirit dictate universal laws to our mind and body rather than trying to impose physical laws to our eternal spirit. We must try to look at the hard times life deals us as a vehicle to teach us to trust in spirit by making choices based on faith, and not on our False Expectations Appearing Real. (Spells FEAR.)

GLOSSARY

Abort Sequence—a term used to describe the barely audible moaning that is a signal to be shaken or awakened in order to reconnect with the physical body.

All That Is—the highest consciousness of all; the Light; the Source; the Creator; God.

Astral Body—or star body; the word *astral* literally means relating to the stars; a containment vehicle for the soul/consciousness, whose very fabric is comprised of astral substance.

Astral Plane—one of the many levels of consciousness that the soul mind can perceive. See Planes of Consciousness.

Astral Travel/Projection—to separate or eject astral matter away from the physical body; this matter can then be used to contain the consciousness.

Dogma—a doctrine or belief that is considered fixed and unchangeable.

Higher Self—the God consciousness in all humans; a type of superconsciousness; the soul mind.

Interrupted Sleep Technique (IST)—a particular sleeping pattern where a person wakes up in the middle of the night, gets up for a couple of hours, then goes back to bed; used to increase the chances of achieving soul travel.

The Light—a term used in books such as *Embraced by the Light* by B. Eadie, *Saved by the Light* by Dannion Brinkley; the Light has been described by near-death experiencers as an angel, Jesus, and sometimes even God.

Mahanta—light giver; one who has achieved the highest state of consciousness, a state of God consciousness; the spiritual leader of Eckankar.

Metaphysics—a philosophy focused on the study of the ultimate causes and foundational nature of things.

Near-Death Experience—usually occurs after an extreme trauma to the body, but sometimes occurs when there is only a danger of loss of life.

Out-of-Body Experience—a term used to describe the consciousness being displaced or projected from the physical body.

Oversoul—an entity or being that has progressed far beyond the limitations of reality as we understand it; a coworker with God.

Paralysis State—also known as night paralysis; the lack of physical mobility after achieving a state of altered consciousness.

Personality Self—a part of the psyche that manages our day-to-day lives; a part of us highly influenced by the ego.

Planes of Consciousness—multiple levels of awareness and/or consciousness labeled the physical, astral, causal, mental, and etheric.

Repeater—a term used to describe the type of soul that is slow or resistant to evolve; a soul that quickly reincarnates without adequate planning; a type D soul on the spiritual arc chart.

Soul Travel—used to describe events similar to out-of-body experiences and astral projection; a term primarily used by the Eckankar Society.

Third Eye—a sometimes dormant ability to see multidimensional realities or substances; an invisible portal or viewport located between the physical eyes.

Training Wheels—a catchall phrase to categorize the techniques and beliefs that are no longer used or required.

Vibration—a rapid oscillation or shaking that appears to be physical but is not; tremors that are usually felt during altered states of consciousness, generally after a significant period of meditation.

White Light—a tool used to protect oneself from negative encounters with one or more nonphysical beings; a type of visualization; a spiritual shield created by the imagination.

REFERENCE BOOKS

Journey of Souls—Michael Newton

Seth Speaks—Jane Roberts

Life Between Life—Joel Whitton

Saved by the Light—Dannion Brinkley

Journeys out of the Body—Robert Monroe

Far Journeys—Robert Monroe

Search for the Truth—Ruth Montgomery

The Education of Oversoul #7—Jane Roberts

The Seth Material—Jane Roberts

Encyclopedia of Ancient and Forbidden Knowledge—Zolar

The Magic Power of Witchcraft—Gavin and Frost

√ *Out on a Limb*—Shirley MacLaine

√ *The Art of Loving*—Eric Fromm

Real Magic—Wayne Dyer

√ *A Course in Miracles*—Foundation for Inner Peace

√ *Ultimate Journey*—Robert Monroe

For More Information

Albert Taylor enjoys hearing from his readers. You can reach him via e-mail at: SolTravler@aol.com, or through Penguin Putnam Inc., attention Audrey LaFehr, 375 Hudson Street, New York, NY 10014. Thanks!

· A NOTE ON THE TYPE ·

The typeface used in this book is a version of Sabon, originally designed in the 1960s by Jan Tschichold (1902–1974) at the behest of a consortium of manufacturers of metal type. As one who began as an outspoken design revolutionary—calling for the elimination of serifs, scorning revivals of historic typefaces—Tschichold seemed an odd choice, but he met the challenge brilliantly: The typeface was to be based on the fonts of the sixteenth-century French typefounder Claude Garamond but five percent narrower; it had to be identical for three different processes, working around the quirks of each, such as linotype's inability to "kern" (allow one character into the space of another, the way the top of a lowercase *f* overhangs other letters). Aside from Sabon, named for a sixteenth-century French punchcutter to avoid problems of attribution to Garamond, Tschichold is best remembered as the designer of the Penguin paperbacks of the late 1940s.